THIS IS HOW IT GOES

Neil LaBute

BROADWAY PLAY PUBLISHING INC
224 E 62nd St, NY NY 10065-8201
212 772-8334 fax: 212 772-8358
BroadwayPlayPub.com

THIS IS HOW IT GOES
© Copyright 2005 by Neil LaBute

First printing: October 2016
I S B N: 978-0-88145-686-8

Book design: Marie Donovan
Typographic controls: Adobe InDesign
Typeface: Palatino
Printed and bound in the U S A

THIS IS HOW IT GOES had its world premiere at the Public Theater in New York City.

CHARACTERS & SETTING

MAN, *thirties*
WOMAN, *thirties*
CODY, *thirties*
WAITRESS, *a woman in her twenties*

Yesterday—a smallish town in the Midwest

I hate the place. I hate the people.
I hate the bloody niggers.
Mustn't call 'em that, you know.
—**Graham Greene**

Nothing fuels a good flirtation
Like need and anger and desperation.
—**Aimee Mann**

I keep a close watch on this heart of mine,
I keep my eyes wide open all the time.
—**Johnny Cash**

For Harold Pinter

(Silence. Darkness)

(A MAN *walks onstage. Let's give him a little light. There, that's better. Now what? Wait—I think he's going to say something.)*

(Yes, he is. Good)

MAN: ...okay. This is how it goes. I mean, went. This is the way it all played out, or is going to. Or *is*...right now. Doesn't matter, you'll figure it out. I think. No, you will...sure you will! No problem. *(Beat)* What you need to know for now, I mean, *right* at this moment, is that there was a girl. 'Course there always is, isn't there? I mean, unless there isn't. Then there's not...but that's pretty self-explanatory. In this one, there's a girl. There's *definitely* a girl.

(Another light up. We need it—a WOMAN *has just appeared. Sitting all alone. For now. The* MAN *glances at her.)*

MAN: Huh. I think I'm gonna go talk to her, because... well, girls are nice. Basically. And that would be enough, but I need to—*talk* with her, I mean. To get this started. Or keep it going...or whatever. You know what I'm saying! Sort of. And which is okay, because *I* only sort of know, too, at this point. *(Beat)* Geez, I think I might end up being an unreliable narrator here...

(The MAN *starts to approach the* WOMAN, *who is seated on a bench. Moves next to her.)*

MAN: ...hello.

(The WOMAN *doesn't react, and the* MAN *snaps his fingers, jumping back to his light spot. What's up? Let's find out.)*

MAN: Just one other thing…I know her. From before. Like, before *now.* So, whether this is happening or, umm, has happened, is all in my head—*however* that works out—I know her already. From school. Okay? Good…I just wanted you to know.

(The MAN *moves back over to the* WOMAN. *Taps her on the shoulder)*

MAN: …hello.

(The WOMAN *turns, looks at the* MAN. *It takes a moment, then she reacts. A lot. She even stands up.)*

WOMAN: Yes? *(Beat)* Oh my God…oh-my-God! Hey, hello. Hi!

MAN: Hello. Again.

WOMAN: Yeah, *again!* Way-way-back again. Wow. Hi!

(Out of nowhere, a hug. Nice. Now we're getting somewhere. The MAN *hugs her right back. Of course)*

MAN: I just…saw you. Saw you sitting there and thought, "Hey". I mean, more than that, more than just "Hey", but that was first. "Hey." You know? "I know her."

WOMAN: Well, good. God, I hope it was more than that!

MAN: No, it was, yeah, it totally was!

WOMAN: Good, because I can't believe it! I can't believe you're just…I mean, standing there. *Right* outside of…

MAN: …Sears. I know, funny, right?

WOMAN: No, more than! It's weird…after, what, like, ten years? To see…

MAN: It's twelve. Yeah. Almost twelve years.

(The WOMAN *looks at the* MAN *again. We might need more light now—some "Sears" light. She gives him another hug.)*

WOMAN: Wow. Really? It's just...wow. About twelve years.

MAN: Yep. A dozen of 'em.

WOMAN: That's...kinda weird.

MAN: Yeah, but not *so* weird, right? Not like we knew each other *super* well or anything...

(The MAN *and the* WOMAN *stand looking at each other for a moment. A voice on the mall intercom interrupts them. They look up, waiting. Then talk again.)*

MAN: ...I just mean...it's okay, too, isn't it? To meet again.

WOMAN: Oh, God, of course, yes. It's good! It is. It's fantastic, but, you know...yeah. It is weird.

MAN: Uh-huh. It definitely has a "weird" flavor. There's a little *weirdness* sprinkled in there...

(The MAN *and the* WOMAN *stop again for a second, looking at each other. That's okay—give 'em some time.)*

WOMAN: ...you look so...I dunno.

MAN: Different?

WOMAN: No, not so much different, 'cause I could recognize you, like, almost instantly. But you're, I dunno...

MAN: What?

WOMAN: Kind of...I mean, you were a lot...

MAN: I was bigger.

WOMAN: ...yes. You were a bigger guy then. In high school.

MAN: I know. I was, wasn't I? Yep. *Big* boy back then!

(The MAN *and the* WOMAN *laugh—what the hell, let's have another hug.)*

MAN: I did some…well, I did R O T C in college, and that was cool. And then, I dunno, I just sort of stopped acting like 7-Eleven was my *kitchen!*

WOMAN: Right…right! You always used to, at lunch, you'd walk down and get those hot dogs, the—

MAN: Two-for-a-dollar ones, exactly! I was, like, you know…that little kid at the movies, remember? The commercial at the drive-in… *(He demonstrates.)* "Two-fisted style!"

WOMAN: I remember that…yes!

MAN: Yeah, it was always right after the dancing candy and soda pop one… *(Beat)* I mean…I think we even went to the movies once, there at the outdoor place that one time. Didn't we?

WOMAN: …did we?

MAN: Yeah, I think. Remember? Over at the…with the paddle- wheel ship out front—what was that called? The…

WOMAN: …Showboat?

MAN: Yes! That's it…some crazy double feature that we all went to. This *group* of us. You don't recall that?

WOMAN: Ummmm, no, I do…I think I do.

(The WOMAN *stops, working to remember this. The* MAN *steps away for a minute. Toward us)*

MAN: …I don't think she does. Not really. I mean, she may say she can, remember us going there, but I don't believe it Girls generally go on more dates and stuff than us guys do at that age, sixteen or so, and that's probably why it's harder to dredge up specific memories. That might be it. 'Cause it really is like yesterday for me. Seriously. It is…

(The MAN walks back over to the WOMAN—she's still thinking. Looks kind of lost while she does this)

WOMAN: Yeah, I think I do, actually. Yes. It was, like, a *comedy* or some…wasn't it?

MAN: Ahh, it was, no. It was *Dances With Wolves*, I think. And then another one…

WOMAN: Oh… *(Frowns)* Well, that had some funny parts…didn't it?

MAN: A couple. Maybe the other one was a comedy, I don't remember.

WOMAN: Yeah, that could be it.

MAN: Right, sure… *(Beat)* So, is that place still open?

WOMAN: What…the Showboat?

MAN: Yeah.

WOMAN: Oh, no…no way! There's, like, a *mall* there now or something. Strip mall—where they have stores but you walk outside. Is that what they call 'em?

MAN: Uh-huh. I think so…I mean, sometimes they come up with a fancier name—Oakbrook Commons or whatnot—but that's basically what they are. *Strip* malls. This long "strip" of stores…

WOMAN: Huh. Well, that was maybe eight years ago they did that. Put in the strip there. *(Beat)* How long since you've been back?

MAN: Oh, you know…

WOMAN: Umm, no, not really.

MAN: No, I mean, I wasn't finished…sorry. I guess, around, ahh, maybe five years. Well, one time about three months ago, just out at the airport—missed a connection, so I was there for a couple hours—but five years, more or less.

WOMAN: …wow. *(Smiles)* Hmmm.

MAN: What? What's so funny?

WOMAN: That was a *lot* of answer for, you know, that one question.

MAN: Sorry! God, yeah, I can go on a little bit...

WOMAN: No, don't be...

MAN: I guess I'm kinda *thorough*...it's the law school in me.

WOMAN: Oh...great! So, you're, I mean...is that your job? "Lawyer"?

MAN: No...'fraid not. That's my ex-job. *Ex*-lawyer. Ex-husband, ex-military. *(Beat)* I'm great at "used to be".

(The WOMAN *laughs at this. An easy laugh. She's loosening up a bit. That's nice.)*

WOMAN: That's funny...I remember now. You were always pretty funny.

MAN: Yeah? Good. Glad you thought that.

WOMAN: Oh, yeah...*everybody* thought you were funny.

MAN: Yep...that's me. *Mr* Comedy. *(Beat)* Anyhow, sorry about going on like that before...blah-blah-blah!

WOMAN: No, I wasn't saying...I mean, it's nice.

MAN: Yeah?

WOMAN: To talk, I mean. About, you know...whatever. Just have a five-minute *conversation* with a person...

MAN: Why, is your husband a mute?

(The WOMAN *looks at him strangely for a moment, without speaking. The* MAN *clears his throat.)*

MAN: I just... God, I hope not! I was kidding. I saw your ring, *noticed* it, and...that's all. *(Beat)* He *can* speak, can't he?

WOMAN: ...rumor has it. Not to *me*, of course, but I know he must. Every so often...

MAN: Ahh. One of those, huh?

WOMAN: Yep. He's a classic. Classic *guy*…

MAN: Ouch. From all of us.

WOMAN: No, sorry, I didn't mean…gosh, listen to me! Listen to me go on like one of those people that you run into…at, like…

MAN: …Sears.

WOMAN: Exactly!

(The WOMAN laughs again—it's a good sound. Then another hug.)

MAN: People're gonna start to talk…

WOMAN: That's okay. Let 'em! Haven't seen you in ten years, so let them say stuff if they want to…

MAN: Twelve. It was twelve years.

WOMAN: Right. Even better…

(The WOMAN lets this thought hang, glancing at her watch. She reacts.)

WOMAN: Oh, damn…can you hold on a sec? I need to…I'm getting a couple keys cut, I need to grab them before five. Just one minute…

(Before the MAN can respond, the WOMAN scurries off. Just disappears. Let's leave the lights up for a bit. I think she'll be back—I think we can trust her.)

MAN: …how great is that? Huh? I came in here for the *baseball card shop*, and I run into her. That's pretty damn nice, I mean…am I being too obvious? 'Cause I really liked her back in school, junior year—hell, even as a senior, she was in my honors English class. And civics, too, I think. Yeah. God, she was something else… *(Remembering)* I used to sit there and watch her, watch her lips moving as she read along with the teacher when we were doing *The Scarlet Letter*. *(Beat)* I know

she's married and all, probably got kids, even, but...
hey, I'm just saying. Whatever. 'S just a little history.

(And then the WOMAN *returns. I told you she would. A
small envelope of keys in one hand.)*

WOMAN: ...hi. Sorry about that.

MAN: Not a problem. *(Points)* You lock yourself out or
something?

WOMAN: What, these? No...it's for a, we have an
apartment. Over the garage. A *garage* apartment...you
know what I mean?

MAN: Ummm...like, an apartment that's above your
garage?

WOMAN: Sorry! Yes...now look who's being thorough!
And *obvious*...

MAN: Right! Thought I was bad...

WOMAN: Uh-huh. Forgive me...comes from being
around a two-year-old.

MAN: Yours?

WOMAN: Of course...a boy.

MAN: No, I didn't mean like you *stole* him or anything,
just...you could be a teacher, for all I know.

WOMAN: Well, that's true. I'm not, but I could be...
could've been a *lot* of things, but I'm the mother of a
great little two- year-old.

MAN: ...plus, a wife.

WOMAN: Yeah. That, too.

MAN: *And* married a mute! Not many people can claim
that...

(That laugh again from the WOMAN. *The* MAN *laughs, too.
Lots of laughs from these two.)*

WOMAN: No, guess not! Not very loudly, anyway...
(Beat) Get it? If I was mute, I couldn't...forget it.

MAN: I never said you were mute.

WOMAN: That's true. Sorry.

MAN: I said you *married* a mute...as far as I'm
concerned, you're perfect.

*(Big pause right here—some cards have just been thrown on
the table. The* WOMAN *is about to respond, thinks better of
it, then looks in the little envelope and counts her keys.)*

WOMAN: Anyway...we've got this thing, this *space* over
the second garage, and we fixed it up. To rent.

MAN: ...nice. Yeah, I'm looking for a place myself.
(Beat) So...two garages, huh?

WOMAN: Uh-huh. He calls it a *guest house*, but it's really
just a bonus room that we... Anyway, it's nice.

MAN: Sounds good. I mean...complicated.

WOMAN: Yeah, my husband just up and...hey,
whatever. It'll be fine. *(Beat)* So, it was great to see you.

MAN: You, too. Seriously.

WOMAN: Yeah, definitely. It definitely was...

MAN: Well, good. Yeah. So...take care.

WOMAN: And you, too! Yeah, you should as well.
Ummm...

MAN: Okay. O-kay. *(Beat)* So, maybe I'll see you at the
strip mall, or...

WOMAN: ...I'm hardly ever over that way.

MAN: I was kidding.

WOMAN: Oh. All right. Because...no, I just thought
that'd be nice. To see you again. At the Wal-Mart there,
or...

MAN: ...Shoe Carnival...

WOMAN: Exactly! That would make me happy. To do that. And there's one of those over there, too, so...

MAN: Well, we're damn near *obligated*, then, aren't we? *(Laughs)* I mean, we could...we can make that happen, I suppose. A strip mall *rendezvous*. *(Beat)* I'm generally pretty free in the daytime...

WOMAN: So, later'd be bad? Just so I know, because...

MAN: No, I was gonna say, followed by evenings *full* of nothing to do. My nights, of course, are absolutely open...

(An ease between the MAN *and the* WOMAN *is starting to build. It feels nice, even from way over here. Comfortable)*

WOMAN: I can always get a sitter. If I need to. My mom or whomever...

MAN: No, we don't have to make it too late...whatever works for you.

WOMAN: Or my husband could watch him. Cody.

MAN: That's cute. Isn't that a really popular kid's name? Cody.

WOMAN: I guess so, but no, that's, no...my son's name is Ralph. Cody's his dad. That's *his* name...

MAN: Huh. Ralph. Well, equally sweet.

WOMAN: Not really, come on...be honest.

MAN: Seriously?

WOMAN: Sure, why not? People should be honest with each other...every twelve years or so.

MAN: Okay, good...that's really hideous. For a child, I mean.

WOMAN: Yeah, I know. *(Beat)* It's his dad's name. *Middle* name, really. One of those family thingies, you know...

MAN: ...in which you had no say.

WOMAN: You must be a great lawyer.

MAN: *Ex*-lawyer.

WOMAN: Right...

MAN: ...and I was only fair at it. Just average. *(Beat)* The Ralph thing was kinda easy.

WOMAN: Really?

MAN: Yeah...I mean, with a dad named Cody.

WOMAN: Well, what can you expect from a *mute*, right?

(This time it's the MAN who laughs first. Quite happily. I'm starting to have high hopes for these two.)

MAN: ...I knew a Cody in school. Our school. That guy who ran track...the runner.

WOMAN: Me, too. I mean...still do.

(The MAN stops in his tracks—well, he's not really moving, but if he were, he'd be stopped in his tracks. He processes.)

MAN: ...oh. That's right, I remember you guys were... so, you *married* Cody Phipps?

WOMAN: That's me...

MAN: Belinda *Phipps*. Huh. Geez.

WOMAN: Wow...you pronounce it like a death sentence.

MAN: Is it?

WOMAN: Umm, no, not really...it's probably pretty regular. As marriages go.

MAN: Great...

WOMAN: ...didn't say it was that. No, it's just...

MAN: ...regular.

WOMAN: Yep.

MAN: Cody Phipps. That's...wild.

WOMAN: Why? *(A bit defensive)* How so?

MAN: Just, you know...I dunno. Well, he was a talker, for one thing. In, like, gym...you couldn't shut the guy up! So, when you said...

WOMAN: Yeah, well, he got a lot quieter...

MAN: Huh. I guess we all do, though. People tend to, in life...

WOMAN: Uh-huh. He got a *lot* a lot quieter.

MAN: I see. *(Checks watch)* Hey, you know what? I need to, umm...

WOMAN: God, I'm sorry, *listen* to me...who cares, right?

MAN: No, it's not that, promise. *(Beat)* I have to pick up some dry cleaning in a minute, that's all...I've got an interview or two this week, so I need...

WOMAN: 'Kay. Anyway...great to see you.

MAN: You, too. Honestly. You look—

WOMAN: Don't say it! It'll never be right.

MAN: Okay. But you do...seriously.

WOMAN: Thank you. You, too.

MAN: ...so, Shoe Carnival it is, then?

WOMAN: Absolutely! When?

MAN: Anytime.

WOMAN: Ahhh, this week. *(Beat)* Ralph needs some new sandals...

MAN: Got it. How about tomorrow, one-thirty?

WOMAN: Great! Okay then...bye.

MAN: Bye. And say hi to, you know...

WOMAN: "Flyin' " Cody Phipps...

MAN: Yep. That's the guy!

WOMAN: I will. See you...

MAN: Goodbye, *Mrs* Phipps...

(A last hug—and it's a nice one. The WOMAN is gone, and those Sears lights fade. The MAN wanders back to his first spot.)

MAN: Cody Phipps. Ho-ly shit...I mean, you know, come on. Come *on*! I can't believe she went and... no, that's not true. I guess you can believe whatever happens in life— there's actually very little that is *un*believable. And I'd heard that they were...but that's way out there. Cody Phipps. Not that he wasn't, you know, popular and stuff, or good- looking, that type of thing...and that dude could run! Damn, could he... He was amazing. Not fast, not so much that, like a lotta those guys are...he didn't *sprint* or anything. No, Cody did all the distances. He would kill you in the long haul, just totally wear you down, then fly right past you...800. 1,200. The 1,500. Cross-country in the fall, which sorta pissed people off because he was great at football, too, but nothing he liked more than running. *(Beat)* Suppose he still is...a runner, I mean. When you like something, a sport, or do a pastime like that, you hardly ever just give it up. Forget about it.

(The lights change to some sort of restaurant. Now there are a table and some chairs—I didn't even notice them before.)

MAN: Why don't we just go meet the guy? Save a little time. You know, I could talk all night or however long we're gonna be here about Cody Phipps—longer about Belinda—but if we were to meet him, just take a second and get acquainted...I think it'd start to help pull this thing all together for you. Okay? Cool...

(The MAN *walks over to one of the chairs, sits. Not long after another man walks in. About the same age. A black guy. He motions toward a* WAITRESS *in the distance.)*

MAN: ...hello, Cody. *(Signals)* Cody?

CODY: Right. Hey, how's it going? Nice to see you. Belinda's coming.

MAN: Good, 'cause I was gonna—

CODY: I mean, she's *right* behind me.

MAN: Great.

(And like CODY *says, here she comes. Belinda. Looking nice, even better than before. More put together. A smile for both men. The marrieds sit down together.)*

CODY: ...so. Hey.

MAN: Yeah, hello. Again.

WOMAN: Hi. Glad the timing all worked out for us to... *(To* CODY*)* I told you he looks different. Doesn't he?

CODY: I guess. I don't really remember you that much. I mean, from class.

MAN: Thanks.

CODY: No, man, no offense, I just don't. Not anybody from then, really, even though we still live here...

MAN: That's all right. 'S the privilege of being rich...

*(*CODY *smiles at this—an easy smile. He doesn't mind being called that. Some things he doesn't like, but this is okay.)*

CODY: Nah, hey, we're not *rich*, we just, you know... take advantage of the ignorant middle class, that's all! *(Beat)* 'S true...take away all the Ralph Lauren and shit, they'd only be hardware stores.

WOMAN: ...comfortable. That's what we are.

MAN: Huh. Anyhow, I do look different.

WOMAN: You really do.

CODY: You're not so fat, right?

(Silence. Then the MAN *bursts out laughing—the* WOMAN *turns white. Whiter than she already is.)*

WOMAN: Cody…

CODY: What? That's it, isn't it? What's the matter with the truth?

MAN: No, you're right, that's pretty much it. I was fatter.

CODY: 'S my point. No big deal.

MAN: Very true, *(To the* WOMAN*)* I thought you said the guy didn't talk much.

(Another silence. The MAN *means it as a joke, but it obviously stings. The marrieds glance at each other.)*

WOMAN: I just meant that…you know…

CODY: You say that?

WOMAN: I wasn't…we were talking about school and all, and I…

CODY: Shit. *(To the* MAN*)* I talk. I just don't *over*talk…

MAN: Got it. See, now, this is the Cody I remember. He always had *plenty* to say…

CODY: Still do, man. I always do. Just say it in my own time…

(On that, CODY *raises a hand to try and catch the eye of the passing* WAITRESS. *She doesn't even pause.* CODY *nods, turns back to the others.)*

CODY: …somebody else might as well try it, 'cause she ain't coming over here for *me*. *(Beat)* Doesn't matter how many shops I open in the area, I'm flat outta luck when it comes to gettin' some *service*…

WOMAN: Honey, I don't think she saw you.

CODY: 'Course she did. She totally saw me. My hand in the air, like a *schoolboy* or something...

MAN: Nah...I think this place always had bad service.

CODY:Yeah? When'd you eat here last?

MAN: Good point. A *decade* or so...

WOMAN: It's okay, I can...

(*The* WOMAN *starts to stand, gets to her feet even, before* CODY *places a hand on her wrist. A firm hand*)

CODY: Just sit. You don't have to do that, go begging...

WOMAN: I'm not, I'm just going to...

CODY: *Sit.* Jesus, just when she comes by again, keep an eye out. Okay?

WOMAN: Sure.

(*The* WOMAN *sits again. Settles herself. A quick glance over at the* MAN.)

MAN: I can go order us all something at the bar, if you guys want...

CODY: No need. She'll be back... (*Smiles*) That's the thing about women, they always come back. Mostly.

MAN: That's a lovely sentiment...

CODY: What?

MAN: ...nothing. I was kidding.

CODY: I wasn't being sentimental. It's true, is all. Women do all kinds of shit, but they usually come back.

WOMAN: Honey, why don't we...?

MAN: Like Lassie, you mean?

CODY: Huh?

MAN: Sorry. Another joke...Lassie was famous for getting home. Returning. I think they even made a movie of it. *Lassie Come Home* or something. And she was a woman…or female dog, anyway.

CODY: …a bitch.

MAN: Well, yeah, technically.

WOMAN: Sweetie…

CODY: What? That's what they're called.

WOMAN: I know, but…people are…

CODY: It's just a word. What's wrong with that? Words only have power if you let 'em…

MAN: Good point. Right.

(The WAITRESS is moving past again. The MAN practically stands up to get her attention. She stops at the table.)

MAN: …hi there. Hey. Could we get, umm, well, just a Coke for me, no ice. And…?

WOMAN: I'd take a lemonade, if that's okay.

CODY: 'Course it's okay, we're gonna pay for it, aren't we? *(To WAITRESS)* And now that you're *here*…water.

(WAITRESS nods and wanders off toward the kitchen. Well, backstage, actually, but we'll pretend there's a kitchen.)

MAN: …I think you made a friend.

CODY: Shit…

WOMAN: That's all Cody drinks is water. Ever since I've known him.

MAN: Yeah?

CODY: Pretty much. 'S good stuff. "Pure. Clean. Feeds the machine." That's what my dad told me, anyway…

MAN: …and it rhymes, which is cool.

CODY: You're kind of a smart-ass, aren't ya? Like, a *jokester*.

MAN: Just a little bit.

CODY: I think I do remember you now. We had P.E. together or something...traded a few rookie cards once.

MAN: Yep. That's right.

CODY: You could play a little dodgeball, but that was about it...

MAN: And "a little" would be stretching it.

CODY: You were okay, for a big kid. Hard as shit to hit, most times...

MAN: ...it was just fear. Purely fear.

CODY: 'S a good game, dodgeball. Yeah.

WOMAN: We never played it...I mean, over on the girls' side of the gym. I think we did a gymnastics unit at that point, or maybe volleyball...

MAN: Huh.

(*A silence seeps into the proceedings. Smiles between the* MAN *and* WOMAN. CODY *looks around for the drinks.*)

MAN: ...so, Cody, you still a runner?

CODY: Yep. Every day.

MAN: Great.

WOMAN: Ten miles...

CODY: Not always. Sometimes I gotta get into the office early, but usually I can burn up ten by breakfast.

MAN: Wow. That's...I mean, I started jogging a little, in the service, but you know, like, two, maybe two and a half's all.

CODY: Hardly break a sweat like that! Not even burning calories till around forty-five minutes...

MAN: Yeah, but I just do it for fun.

CODY: *Fun?*

MAN: Sort of. Got hooked on it... *(Beat)* We should go sometime.

CODY: ...I don't do nothing for fun.

WOMAN: Cody, come on... *(To the* MAN*)* That is not true. He's...

CODY: What? What do I do that's fun...or "for" fun?

WOMAN: Umm...oh, you know. Just stuff. All people have fun.

MAN: I do.

CODY: Well, then, we're different people, aren't we?

MAN: That is true.

WOMAN: Ahhh...you help out at the school. With track. That's fun, isn't it?

CODY: Yeah, but it's...no. It's helping out. I mean, yes, I *like* it, but I don't do it for fun. I coach a few runners, that's not, like, some big *hobby* or anything...

MAN: That's great. Give a little back...

CODY: ...that would imply that they gave me something in the first place.

MAN: Touché.

*(*CODY *and the* MAN *look at each other—a smile between them. It's one of those guy things; better just leave it be.)*

WOMAN: What about your golf?

CODY: Please...that's business. I do that 'cause these Midwestern dudes love it, so out I go...once they let me on the course, I mean.

*(*CODY *seems happy to pursue this subject when the* WAITRESS *returns, dropping off the drinks. Not a word out of her.)*

MAN: ...she seems very sweet.

WOMAN: Right! *(Laughs)* A lovely young woman.

CODY: Yeah, de-light-ful.

(The MAN *smiles at this and takes a sip. So does the* WOMAN. CODY *looks around the restaurant as the* MAN *suddenly stands.)*

MAN: ...I think this is Diet. Lemme run it up front, it'll be faster.

CODY: Give 'em hell...

MAN: Yep, that's me. The Hellraiser... *(Gestures)* If my head was shaved, you could see the *pins* and everything! *(Beat)* You know, the movie with the guy who's all...I'll be right back.

(The MAN *smiles and moves back into his original light. Looks out at us)*

MAN: ...I gotta be honest. That was a total line I just threw out there, the Diet Coke thing. Yeah. See, I thought it was getting a little bit uncomfortable, didn't you? Uh-huh. Kind of, anyway. So I just wanted to take a sec and regroup here...

(The MAN *looks back over at* CODY *and the* WOMAN. *They sit in silence, maybe a perfunctory word or two.)*

MAN: Is it me, or does he seem a little pissed off? I totally get that vibe from him. Pissed right off about something. *(Beat)* He didn't always used to be that way, not when I knew him, anyhow. Not that we were, like, tight or anything. Best buds. But I knew him enough...enough to say that much about him, and he never seemed so keyed up like this. I mean, maybe after his mom left, for a while there he was kinda...you know. How you get when that sort of thing happens. You're just cruising along and then, wham! Life gets, like, all shitty. Matter of minutes...I think that's what happened to him. And, thing is, she'd do it about every other *month*. Plus there's the whole race thing...not that he made a huge deal about it at school, but yeah, he

pulled that card out a few times back then. Just once
or twice a *day*! Nobody really called him on it, but it
was completely obvious when he'd do it. School lunch
line, picking teams for gym, when some girl or other
wouldn't go out with him…like, *whenever* he needed
some excuse, basically. We used to call it the ol' "Ace 'a
Spades". I mean, not to his face, God no, you kidding?
Cody was, well, you know…kinda fierce. Pretty
serious when he wanted to be, so no. We'd say it when
we were alone, just a few of the guys. Say, like, "Hey,
Cody just whipped out the Ace 'a Spades". And that's
when somebody'd say, one of my friends would…
"Just gotta call a spade a spade". *(Smiles)* We were only
just joking, but it was pretty funny. At the time…

(The MAN *looks to us for validation—does he get any? Well,
we'll have to see. For now let's imagine that it remains silent
out there. He nods, then turns back toward the table.)*

MAN: I'm gonna head back over now…new drink
wouldn't really take all that long to get, right?

(The MAN *nods to us, then turns and moves back to his
chair. Sipping from his old drink as he arrives.)*

MAN: …I was right.

CODY: Yeah? Looks like the same thing…

MAN: Well, it's a Coke glass. They all have the same
kind of…

CODY: No, the color of it. Seems a little light, like the
last one did.

MAN: Huh. No, it's…

WOMAN: Does it taste okay?

MAN: Yeah! Just fine, thanks…

WOMAN: Great.

MAN: 'S a classic taste, isn't it?

WOMAN: Yes, I love it. The original one.

CODY: I wouldn't know. Don't drink soft drinks…no *pop* for me.

MAN: That's good.

CODY: Why?

MAN: Well, you know…

CODY: No, what? It's just a choice.

MAN: Yeah, but a pretty healthy one. I mean—

CODY: Whatever. *(Beat)* So…what brings you back to town?

MAN: Umm, this and that. Stuff. How's that for vague?

CODY: Pretty good. You nailed it. So?

WOMAN: Cody, if he doesn't want to…

MAN: No, I'll talk about it, that's…not much to "talk" about in that sense, really. I'm just moving back. I miss it.

CODY: …yeah? You miss *this* place?

MAN: I do.

CODY: Huh.

WOMAN: That's nice. You know? To miss the town where you…people don't care enough about their roots, I don't think.

MAN: I agree. It's easy to forget what's important. Where you come from.

WOMAN: I know, it really is. *Roots*…

CODY: What do you mean by that?

MAN: I think she's saying you should move back to Africa…

(Big silence on this one. Remember how I said there are certain things CODY *doesn't like? This would be one of them.)*

CODY: ...man, that is not cool.

MAN: It's a *joke. (Beat)* I mean, come on, Cody, I was just..."Words only have power if you let them." Right?

WOMAN: Honey, I don't think he meant to—

CODY: No, hey, whatever. Come to meet a guy, allow him to move into my *home,* and he insults me, that's fine. If you don't mind that, ho-ney, then that's fine...

MAN: I didn't...it wasn't meant as a hurtful thing. God, no! I was just trying to be funny. *(Beat)* Sorry.

WOMAN: I think we're all just a little tense. Nervous.

CODY: I'm not nervous, why would I be nervous? Hmm?

WOMAN: I dunno, maybe...you know.

CODY: No. I don't know. I've got this nice new studio over my garage, and I'm looking for a tenant. Not some asshole.

MAN: Cody, honestly...forgive me. It was just a...she said "roots", and it popped into my head. That's—

CODY: Oh.

MAN: The show, that's all. With the dad from *Good Times* and, you know, that dancer...somebody Vereen. *(Beat)* There was no disrespect meant. It was a mistake...

CODY: Fine.

WOMAN: It's okay.

CODY: Hey. *(Looks at* WOMAN*)* Don't you do that. Don't apologize for me, or go saying that something is okay. Got that? Do- not. I said it was fine, not that it was okay. *Big,* big difference...

WOMAN: I'm sorry. Cody, please, I—

MAN: What's the difference?

CODY: What?

MAN: No, I mean, you said something about the difference between "fine" and "okay", and I'm trying to think what it is.

CODY: Dude, just leave it.

MAN: All right. Just trying to…

WOMAN: Why don't we…

CODY: You know what "okay" means, means that it's okay. It's *all* all right. And "fine" is something else. Says, "Yeah, I'll let it go". *I'm* letting it go. Fine. But it is not o-kay.

(They all take long, uncomfortable sips from their beverages. The WAITRESS *passes again. Oblivious. Doesn't see* CODY *raise his hand.)*

CODY: …and that shit is not "okay", either! What is it with her?

MAN: You got me. *(Beat)* Do you need something?

WOMAN: She's probably trying to cover too many tables…I used to work here back whenever, in school, *(To the men)* Do you remember that?

MAN: Depends. Do you remember me sitting in that corner booth there, almost every day after school?

WOMAN: …I do. With your homework.

MAN: Yep!

CODY: I never came in here. Least not back then, anyhow. And not after school. I had sports…

MAN: Right, 'course you did.

CODY: Yeah.

WOMAN: It was always quiet then, around four or so, before the dinner rush...and you'd be over there reading and sipping on a drink.

MAN: Uh-huh. And probably a basket of cheese fries, too! I was a *porker* in those days...God.

CODY: Yep. You were kind of a tubby sorta guy then, weren't you?

MAN: Oh yeah.

CODY: And with the wise mouth, too.

MAN: You are correct, sir.

CODY: Surprised you didn't get picked on more...beat up and shit.

MAN: I got my share, don't worry. There was plenty of that...

WOMAN: That's awful.

MAN: Nah, made me a better person. It's what I told myself, anyway, lying there in *traction*...

WOMAN: Oh my God. *(Beat)* Really?

CODY: No, that's bullshit.

MAN: 'Course it is. But I did get a few bumps in my day...the occasional *undies* up the flagpole.

(CODY *laughs at this, the first time we've heard that. It seems out of place, almost frightening.*)

MAN: ...well, now I know who was behind *that*.

CODY: No, man, sorry, but, I can remember it. Seriously. Seeing your Fruit of the Looms flapping up there, all the way down by the track! Certain times... that was funny.

(CODY *laughs halfheartedly again, but it's passed now. Over)*

CODY: Anyway, whatever. So what's the deal? You want the place or not?

MAN: Ummm...

WOMAN: Honey, he'd probably like to see it first. *(To the* MAN*)* Right?

MAN: Yeah, that'd be—

CODY: Why? I mean, it's new. All the stuff in there is *new*, so what's the problem?

MAN: Nothing, no, just that it's, you know...furnished.

CODY: So?

MAN: So, I'd like to see if my things'll go with...I dunno. The *carpet*...

CODY: Oh. Okay, fine, if you're like *that* about it, all *particular*, then okay. Do it. Check it out.

MAN: Thanks.

WOMAN: It's pretty nice. We did it all in neutrals. You know, with whites and creams and that sort of—

MAN: Great. I'll take a look. And it's how much...six-fifty?

CODY: Yep. *(Beat)* I was planning to knock it down if somebody wanted to do a little yard work for me...

WOMAN: Cody, we never—

CODY: I know, I know, I'm joking! I can *joke*, too, can't I?

MAN: Sure. No, I'd make a hell of an indentured servant...you're right.

CODY: I'm not talking about no servant. If you do some gardening, you get paid. That's all. *(To the* WOMAN*)* Did the same thing with that one student, the exchange student. Remember?

(The WOMAN *nods, then takes a sip. Quiet for a moment. That's okay, they all need a breather.)*

MAN: Sure. I know, I get it. And I'm not above that... *(Beat)* Beggars can't be...well, you know.

CODY: Exactly.

MAN: Great.

WOMAN: Well, that's really nice...we can set a time to take a look later.

MAN: Perfect.

CODY: ...and why're you here again? Back in town, I mean?

MAN: Just, you know...getting back to basics. Simplifying. *(Beat)* Wasn't so big on the corporate thing, all the wheeling and dealing I had to do, that sorta stuff. I'm no lawyer, that's what I found out. 'Course, I had to go to law school and take on about seventy *thousand* in loans to figure it out, but hey!

(They all chuckle at this—kind of vacantly, but they're trying.)

MAN: Anyhow, I'm cutting back, gonna do some writing that I always wanted to do, and...

WOMAN: That sounds good...

CODY: Sort of like that Grisham, huh?

MAN: What, you mean...John Grisham?

CODY: Yeah, he did that, right? Stopped being a lawyer and became a writer.

MAN: Uh-huh. Yes, like that. Except for the theater... I'm gonna be a—

CODY: Well, that's cool...lawyers are pretty good at making shit up. I know *mine* are! *(Laughs)* Great.

WOMAN: ...that's exciting...

MAN: Yep. Might have to sell a bit of my card collection for cash, but…

CODY: Yeah…seriously?

MAN: Maybe. Thought I'd…

CODY: You still got that Jackie Robinson you took off me? Huh?

MAN: Hey, I didn't "take" it off you, you traded it…

CODY: Yes, but…

MAN: Fair and square, *(To the* WOMAN*)* Guy is still sore about that!

CODY: 'S my favorite card.

MAN: Then you should've kept it…

CODY: Right.

WOMAN: What is it…a baseball card?

MAN: Uh-huh. It's one he gave me back in school. For a favor.

WOMAN: Wow…that doesn't sound like Cody. Asking for *help* from somebody…

CODY: Yeah, well, I needed it. *(Beat)* It was a sweet card, too.

MAN: I know. 1952 Topps. Mint condition, *(To the* WOMAN *again)* You know why there are so few Robinson cards from that time?

WOMAN: Uh-uh. Why?

CODY: Because people destroyed 'em. Dads, their kids, folks would get them—white folks, that is—find them in their gum pack and rip the fuck out of 'em because the dude was a black man, this uppity black who somehow snuck his way onto a ball team…that is why. Guys across America were tearing his picture up to show that they did not like it. Rookie of the year,

M V P, they still didn't give a shit. And that's why it's so damn rare...

WOMAN: ...and that's why you want it?

CODY: You don't get it. *(To the* MAN*)* She doesn't get shit like this. Never has...

MAN: That's okay. It's pretty much a guy thing... *(To the* WOMAN*)* It's not just that, anyway. This one had a flaw in it. 'S a misprint that—

CODY: Whatever. *(Beat)* You serious about it, I'll swing a deal with you.

MAN: Maybe. I'm probably gonna need to do something...actually, as long as I can pay the child support, I'm okay...

WOMAN: Oh. Oh! I wasn't...I mean, I didn't know you had kids. That's...great.

MAN: *Kid.* Just the one. A girl.

CODY: Where's she at?

MAN: My daughter? Oh, she's, you know, with her mom.

CODY: Man, I could never give up my kids.

(This reference is caught by the MAN—*he and the* WOMAN *should share a brief look—before he goes on.)*

MAN: I didn't give 'er up...I see her all the time. It's just...

CODY: Complicated, I'm sure. Always is. Raising kids isn't complicated, you ain't doing it right... *(Beat)* But hey, that's your business.

*(*CODY *stands, stretches, then puts out a hand.)*

CODY: I gotta go, need to swing past the store over on Tamarack. Replaced a manager, so...

(The MAN *stands, along with the* WOMAN. CODY *and his wife hold a look for a moment.)*

CODY: Good to see you. And look, you two work out a time to check the place and make a decision or not on the, you know, *carpet... (Shakes hands with the* MAN*)* See ya.

MAN: Yeah, you, too.

WOMAN: Bye, sweetie.

*(*CODY *and the* WOMAN *kiss.)*

WOMAN: Talk to you later.

*(*CODY *nods as he drops a wad of cash on the table. Exits)*

MAN: ...well. That was...huh.

WOMAN: Yeah. Sorry.

MAN: No, totally fine, just not what I was expecting. It got a little hot there for a minute...

WOMAN: I know. Yes.

MAN: So..."kids", huh? You didn't say that before. *Kids*. How come?

WOMAN: Oh, you know...because.

MAN: No, why?

WOMAN: ...because he hates me. Cody *Jr*. He's *six*, and he pretty much hates me. *(Beat)* I'll just pay for the...

(The WOMAN *tries to smile but just misses pulling it off. She grabs the money and heads to the counter. The* MAN *is alone.)*

MAN: ...anyway, it was more or less like that. I'm not *completely* sure she said his name then, her other son's, but she might've. Probably did. And, so, that's how I got into the apartment over the garage. I mean, I may've walked her out to her car, or am going to—I still don't get the time thing here!—but it basically

happened that way. Cody all tense and whatever, and
me just trying to stay out of the way. Her, too. Belinda,
I mean. Yeah, I get the feeling that she needs to stay out
of the way a lot…or, as she said earlier (or will later), a
lot a lot. Yeah…

*(Lights need to pop up now on another playing area—turns
out we're going to need a few. This one should be some kind
of nice sitting-room area. Just a few pieces to suggest it.
We'll fake the rest.)*

MAN: We should probably keep moving now. Most of
you'll need to get on home after this, right? I'm sure
you do. Even if you have no one to get home to, you
still need to get there… Okay, good. Now, I'm not
going to be in this next bit, I mean, I will in *spirit* or
whatever, because I'll be talked about, things like that,
but I won't actually be there. Don't worry, though, no
big deal, I'm gonna be back…maybe just imagine I'm
up in the apartment there…fixing my lunch or reading
some book, that kind of thing. Making notes. I may
even have myself a little job by this point—I do end up
helping out with the yard work—so, something along
those lines. But this part right now is pretty important
to the rest, so do pay attention… 'Kay? Fine. *(Beat)* If
you don't, you'll never find out how Belinda ends up
with the black guy…"eye", I mean "black *eye*"! Geez,
that's a Freudian slip, huh? *(Chuckles)* Like I said, I
wasn't there, so I didn't see it—or won't—but *you* get
to see it all. If you pay attention. All I know is later,
when Cody's out at the office, she comes to me, and I
see it and freak out a bit, but she never actually tells me
about what happened. Not really. *(Beat)* So, this is how
it goes. This part. Okay, I'll shut up now…

*(The MAN smiles and backs off, disappearing just as the
WOMAN enters. She plops onto the couch after putting a
baby monitor down on the coffee table. Sorry—yeah, we 'll*

need a coffee table, too. She has a magazine and a diet cola with her.)

WOMAN: ...hello? *(Beat)* I'm in here!

CODY: *(Offstage)* Why? Why're you in there?

WOMAN: I just...because.

(CODY enters, drenched in sweat from working out. Nike shirt, shorts. Maybe even wearing sunglasses. He looks pretty cool.)

CODY: 'Cause why? Huh? Why do you always hole up in this room, way the other side of the house?

WOMAN: Cody, I like it in here. It's sunny during the morning, and I can relax a minute when the baby's asleep...

CODY: Hey, he's not a baby, okay? Kid is two years old...you *treat* him like a baby, but he's not.

WOMAN: Listen, he needs to—

CODY: No, you listen. What he doesn't need is taking a nap at eight in the morning! All right? He just got up, like, an hour and a half ago. And you give 'im breakfast and back to bed he goes...that's wrong.

WOMAN: He's tired. He's—

CODY: No, you're lazy, that's what it is.

WOMAN: "Lazy"?

CODY: You heard me. Yeah. You get Cody Junior off to school— great—and put a little food down Ralph, and then that's it for the day, far as you think...

WOMAN: That is not...

CODY: Bullshit! Bull-shit. I know it is.

WOMAN: Cody, our son is tired, do you mind? I know *you* don't get that way, since you run every day and never come to bed before, say, *two* in the morning...

but other people, we sleep. He's a child. A growing
boy, and he needs a nap whenever he feels like it. Right
now, an hour from now...whenever.

(CODY *shakes his head and pulls off his shirt, flexing. Does a
few stretches. Yes, he s in good shape.)*

CODY: That shit is abuse...

WOMAN: What?! I mean, why would you even say...?

CODY: It is! You ever hear of *raising* children? Huh?
You raise them, they don't do it themselves... You're
the parent, you set the rules, make the choices. Not the
kid.

WOMAN: And when was the last time you took part in
that? "Raising" him. Hmm?

CODY: Don't start that crap...I work.

WOMAN: Oh, please...

CODY: What?! I do, 's more than you can say.

WOMAN: Cody! I mean...

CODY: ...hey, truth hurts.

WOMAN: *(To herself)* God...this is like a Thomas Hardy
novel or something.

CODY: The fuck does that mean?

WOMAN: ...that's kinda *Victorian*, don't you think? "I
work." I mean, come on...we both work, I just happen
to work *here.* In this house of yours. I mean, your
father's—

CODY: It's my house. *My* house. 'Kay? He's dead and
this is mine. Including this room here, which you know
I hate you being in...

WOMAN: *Why?!*

CODY: Because it's a sitting room, okay? "Sitting."
Supposed to be for the evening, or when you have
guests over…

WOMAN: No, it's not.

CODY: Yeah, it is. Yes! You go read one of those
Architectural Digests or something I have in the den, it'll
tell you the same damn thing…

WOMAN: Who cares?

CODY: I do. I care! You sitting in here, middle of the
morning, with your feet up and sucking down that
damn Tab you drink all the time…looks lazy. You look
like a fuckin' pig, and I hate it!

WOMAN: Wow. Okay, that's…well, that's a new
one. I mean, you've usually got something *lousy* to
say to me, but that there is a completely new one.
Congratulations…

CODY: Shut up.

WOMAN: Nice comeback…

CODY: Fuck that. I don't need a *comeback*. I need a wife
who doesn't park it on her fat ass all day, sucking on
pop like she's some sixteen-year-old…

WOMAN: I wish I was.

CODY: What?

WOMAN: That. Sixteen…

CODY: Yeah, why's that?

WOMAN: …because that was the year *before* I met you.
Okay? That's why…

*(The WOMAN can see CODY react at this, but she can't
stop now. Not very wise, maybe, but that's how it goes
sometimes.)*

CODY: …well, well.

WOMAN: Co-dy...I'm just saying... (*Thinks*) I always liked you because you were different, you know? Back whenever. But now, I mean, now you're just so worried about somebody giving you shit, or disrespecting you, or I don't know what...and it's not about that. Black or white or any of that crap. It's about being a good guy, Cody. A *decent* person. And you're not...in the end, I'm with somebody who's like all the other guys I grew up around. Not so terrible, but not very good, either. You're just a guy. Just a *normal* guy...which means kind of shitty, actually. Completely average and a little bit shitty.

(CODY *tenses up, turns to her. He starts to advance slowly, wrapping his shirt around his hand—like a boxer wraps tape around his fist before putting it in the glove. The* WOMAN *stands, facing him.*)

CODY: 'S that right?

WOMAN: Cody, look...I didn't mean...

CODY: Is it? Great. That's really great.

WOMAN: ...I wasn't being...don't...

CODY: No, that's funny. You're getting real cute with your mouth lately. Must be your little friend over the garage there, making you all clever and smarty-pants like that...

WOMAN: He hasn't been...no. I was just trying to say that—

CODY: ...make another wish. Go ahead...one more.

(CODY *continues to move toward the* WOMAN *as she backs away. Finally, she comes up against a love seat and is trapped. She looks at him, shit scared. I mean, come on, wouldn't you be? She tries to reach out and touch him. He pulls back. She is starting to cry. Shaking her head*)

CODY: Go on...make one.

WOMAN: …I wish…you wouldn't hurt me.

CODY: Huh. *(Beat)* Too late…

(CODY smacks the WOMAN flat in the stomach, doubling her over. She drops to her knees and disappears behind the small couch. He reaches down and hits her again, this time in the face. We can't see exactly what happens, but the sound is sickening. For a moment, silence. Then the sound of a child waking up on the baby monitor. CODY unwraps his hand and starts off.)

CODY: I'll get 'im. *(Beat)* You better put something on that eye. Try your *soda pop* there…that's nice and cold.

(CODY exits. The room is empty, the WOMAN still behind the piece of furniture. After a moment, the MAN enters the room. What's he doing here again?)

MAN: …okay, so maybe it wasn't *exactly* like that. I dunno. Hey, look, I'm a writer—would-be writer, anyway—so, what can I tell ya? I've got a hell of an imagination, and I just go with it sometimes…listen, it could've happened that way! Easily—I mean, she did get the eye once, this black eye, and so, I'm just guessing. That's all. Actually…it's probably how I *want* it to be, like, so I can jump in there, save her or whatever. That's probably it…but still, this might've been a touch of an exaggeration. Yeah. Anyway, all stories need some sort of antagonist, don't they? Sure. Someone to dislike, or you want to see fail or whatever…well, I figure I'm gonna have to play the ol' Ace 'a Spades on that one! Yep. Only choice I've got…I mean, it can't be me. And not her, I don't want it to be her, so…Cody's the guy. *(Beat)* But to be fair, I have no idea if it happened that way or not. The bruise thingie. No…that was probably a bit much, we should go ahead and give it another try.

(Suddenly, the WOMAN walks back into the room—how did she get out there? Well, it should seem pretty magical, but

*it'll need to be a theatrical trick. A trapdoor or something.
Anyhow, she walks back in, same as before, except this time
holding the Tab can to her eye and carrying the magazine.
She sets down the baby monitor and plops onto the couch.)*

MAN: What I'm saying is, this is the way *she* described
it to me, Belinda did, after it occurred. But, see, umm, I
didn't really believe her…I mean, she *swears* it was this
way, she does, but something seems a little off about it,
and so that's why I made up the other story. The first
one. Look, you decide for yourselves. *(Beat)* Anyway,
sorry about that. Told you before that you shouldn't
totally trust me on any of this!…

(The MAN *smiles and exits. After a moment, the* WOMAN
calls out.)

WOMAN: …hello? *(Beat)* I'm in here.

CODY: *(Offstage)* Why? Why're you in there?

WOMAN: I just…because.

*(*CODY *walks in, back from a run. Dressed the same as before
but not nearly as sweaty. Wearing the sunglasses up on his
head. He moves over toward the* WOMAN.*)*

CODY: …hey. *Hey.* What happened?

WOMAN: Oh, nothing, no, I just…I left the cupboard
door open and…

CODY: Baby, oww. Ouuw! Lemme see…

*(*CODY *crouches beside the* WOMAN, *lifting the soda can to
have a peek at his wife's condition.)*

CODY: Damn…

WOMAN: Bad?

CODY: Mmm-hmm. Gonna be…

WOMAN: Great. *(Touches it)* Ouuuh…

CODY: Hey, I'm the one who should be grumpy…the person who's gonna suffer is me. The shit I'll get for this'll be unbelievable…

WOMAN: S'pose so. *(Beat)* Good…

CODY: People'll be saying I smacked you one. They totally will… *(Beat)* "Black man goes on rampage", shit like that.

(CODY laughs at this, as does the WOMAN. She winces from the pain. He reaches over and kisses her gently.)

CODY: There. Daddy'll make it all better.

WOMAN: Mmmmm…

CODY: You should probably use some ice, though. Honey? You should. Way more helpful than that soda pop…

WOMAN: I know, but…

CODY: You want me to get some?

WOMAN: Yeah, but…in a minute. 'Kay?

CODY: Sure.

(CODY pulls off his sweaty shirt and stretches—still looks good. He plops down on the couch near the WOMAN, lifting up her legs and then pulling them onto his lap. She smiles.)

WOMAN: Thanks… *(Beat)* So, how're your protégés coming?

CODY: Hmmm? Oh, they're, you know…don't know if they'll make state, but…working hard.

WOMAN: That's good.

CODY: Yeah.

WOMAN: Nice of you to…you know, help out.

CODY: Least I can do. I mean, I dump a ton 'a cash into that program, new *uniforms* and shit…might as well make sure some of the runners get their shot at a scholarship or, you know. Right?

WOMAN: Sure. That's… Sure.

CODY: Absolutely. *(Beat)* Baby's okay?

WOMAN: Yeah, he's sleeping…

CODY: Good. That's cool. I know he's not feeling well, so…

WOMAN: What time do you have to go in?

CODY: Got a meeting at ten. Should be there a bit before…

WOMAN: Why?

CODY: You know, check in with everybody, do my e-mails and shit.

WOMAN: Oh. Okay.

CODY: …what? *What?*

WOMAN: Nothing. I just…I was hoping you could take today off, it's Friday and, you know, it'd just be…we talked about you taking Fridays off once in a while.

CODY: Yeah, but…

WOMAN: No, I understand. We were gonna do the picnic thing with…but hey. *(Beat)* Who're you meeting with?

CODY: So tell 'em we'll get together and do something next week. 'S not a big deal. *(Beat)* It's some people in from Chicago. Those, uhh, you know…I told you.

WOMAN: No…

CODY: …yeah, I did. The one guy's from, I don't know the place—Arlington Heights or whatever—they have the plant out there we want to use for that new line…

WOMAN: Oh.

CODY: ...the Adirondack line we're gonna add. All the furniture. Remember? *(Beat)* I told you.

WOMAN: Did you?

CODY: Yes.

WOMAN: Huh. Well, I must've forgot...

CODY: Yeah. You just forgot or something, 'cause I told you.

WOMAN: 'Kay.

(CODY kisses the WOMAN on her bare feet and stands, wiping his neck with the rumpled shirt.)

CODY: I'm gonna hop in the shower...get myself ready. *(Beat)* Hey, tell our *tenant* to mow that side yard today, would ya? I think he missed it last time...

WOMAN: All right. *(Beat)* That's a new one...

CODY: What's that?

WOMAN: Showering before work.

CODY: What do you mean?

WOMAN: I mean that you don't usually do that. Shower. Not before work, anyway...

CODY: Yeah, I do.

WOMAN: Uh-uh. Not usually...I mean, not if you've just been out with the team. Timing them or whatever.

(CODY, exasperated, throws his shirt on the end of the couch. Comes over and hovers, leaning in dangerously close to the WOMAN.)

CODY: Look...

WOMAN: I'm just saying...just saying it, that's all.

CODY: Well, don't, okay? We do not need all this jealousy crap. 'Kay?

WOMAN: Fine. That's fine, Cody, whatever.

(CODY *leans down a little closer to the* WOMAN, *letting her get a good sniff.)*

CODY: ...there, how's that? *(Holds her head)* No, no, go on, take a whiff. Nice, huh?

WOMAN: ...all right...

CODY: No, seriously, a little more. Okay? You smell that? I'm nasty right now, got clients coming, so just do not get into your Desdemona shit. Have people to meet, that's all...

WOMAN: Go, then. Should be nice...have a great lunch. Make a bundle.

CODY: There is just no talking to you...

WOMAN: Yeah, well, I sorta like the truth tossed in there every now and then when I'm chatting with a person...I'm just funny that way.

CODY: Oh shit...I'm outta here.

WOMAN: Yep. Go. Maybe we'll have the food without you... *(Beat)* ...go on.

(CODY *throws his hands in the air—there really is no talking to the* WOMAN *some days. This seems to be one of them.)*

CODY: Yeah, I will. So I can make us some more money. Mo-ney that you have no problem spending...

WOMAN: I just spend it to piss you off.

CODY: Well, hey, it works!

WOMAN: Good...

CODY: Yep, great. You have a *super* day, ho-ney...

WOMAN: I will. Thanks. And tell her hi for me... whoever she is. *This* time.

CODY: You are, like, so nuts...I mean it. Just completely crazy.

WOMAN: Well, be proud of yourself, 'cause you made me this way...

CODY: No, uh-uh, that is bullshit...total shit, and I'm not taking the fall on this one. *(Beat)* You were pretty fucking out there when I first knew you, all the way back at school, but I *dealt* with it, that's what I did.

WOMAN: That's great...

CODY: You take the hand you're dealt, 's what my old man always said, and so I did it. And you, sweetness, were just one of the cards God threw my way...

WOMAN: I really don't know what the hell you just said, but I'm sure it means something to you...

CODY: You know exactly what I'm saying...

WOMAN: No, Cody, I don't. I really don't.

(CODY moves closer to the WOMAN. Towering over her. She tries to hold her own, but hey, let's be honest. This guy can be a bit unnerving.)

CODY: I'm saying that, had I been mature enough in high school to see past your *bangs* and your cute little cheerleader skirt, shit like that...I probably wouldn't be standing here, having this stupid fucking talk with you. Because you would not be in my house...

WOMAN: Yeah? Well, I am now...but *you* can go. Just tell me when and I'll help you pack up, have you outta here in under an hour.

CODY: I am not going nowhere.

WOMAN: Well, that's a double negative, but I get your point...

CODY: I bet you do. I bet you do at that. And I get yours...

WOMAN: ...and so there we are. Same lousy place we usually find ourselves at.

CODY: Yep.

WOMAN: Great. That's really great…

(CODY *starts off but stops, catching himself. Simmering*)

CODY: Yeah, super. *(Beat)* Okay, fine, you wanna know the truth? Huh? Who I'm seeing on the side, 's that it? My work, that's who. She's my fucking mistress…

WOMAN: …right…

CODY: It's true. I like it, I'm good at it, and it makes me happy. I *love* making more money than any other guy in this town, 'cause it just pisses 'em off. I dig that. Plus, work doesn't complain, or rag on me about shit, or leave those fucking *tampons* wrapped in toilet paper in the trash for the dog to drag down to the living room…so, yeah, I love my work. I LOVE it, and there is not a damn thing that you can do about it… *(He flicks his shirt at the wall. Exhales loudly)* This sucks. You know that? This whole thing, what we've got here…or ended up with. It really sucks. It's shit…

WOMAN: No. It's *marriage.*

(CODY *is about to respond when a child begins to whimper on the baby monitor. The parents look at each other.*)

WOMAN: …So?

CODY: Hey, you're always saying "We both work, I just work here". So, get to *work*… *(He makes a dismissive gesture with his hand. Does it again)* Don't forget to tell Shakespeare to cut the grass…

(And with that, CODY *is gone. The* WOMAN *sits for a moment, taking all this in. A long moment. Then she starts to cry. Not a lot—that's hard on an actor, and we've got a ways to go—but a little. Just enough)*

WOMAN: *(To herself)* …it was *Othello* who was jealous! Not the other way around. Asshole.

(The lights fade on her and up slowly on the MAN, *who is now standing in his old spot. He's changed his clothes—not too much, but khakis and a shirt, tennis shoes—and seems ready to go somewhere.)*

MAN: ...see what I mean? I don't really know the whole story, but those two have got something going on. Some sorta trouble. They do... *(Beat)* I mean, it's a *detached* garage and all, but hey...voices carry.

(Lights slowly rise on a new playing space while the MAN *is talking. A sort of backyard, with maybe a barbecue pit or that type of thing. A picnic table. We won't use it just yet, but I wanted to give you a heads-up.)*

MAN: ...we're gonna be together again in a minute—the three of us, I mean—so I just wanted to grab a second here and sort of set this up, let you know what's going on. By the way, funny how you never see the kids, isn't it? It's not weird or anything, like in *Virginia Woolf* or whatever...it's just a personal choice. We thought that might be too much, plus kids're hard as shit to work with—not them themselves, I mean, I like kids, I do—but the labor laws and tutors and all that crap, so we just decided against 'em. Or plan to, after this gets finished and somebody decides to stage the thing...anyhow, what I'm saying is: Children are great, but you ain't gonna see any of 'em tonight! Okay? Good.

*(*CODY *and the* WOMAN *enter now, each taking up positions in the backyard space,* CODY *is manning the grill, and she is busy setting the table. Plates, forks, napkins. That sort of deal. The* MAN *looks over at them and smiles.)*

MAN: ...they really are a pretty great-looking couple. I mean, when you just see them together, from afar. Problem is, I think it has to be *really* afar, because otherwise you might hear what they're saying to each other! Still, they are very attractive people...and in a way, that makes all this somewhat, umm, sadder. Not that I...well, watch what happens. You'll see what I mean. Sorry! I'm being so *cryptic*, and I don't mean to be. Just watch. It's all gonna be okay in the end. It will, I promise...

(The MAN *smiles out at us and then moves off, toward* CODY *and the* WOMAN. *They spot him coming—*CODY *turns back to his grill, and the* WOMAN *stands to greet the* MAN. *They hug;* CODY *catches it.)*

MAN: ...hello!

WOMAN: Oh! Hi there...

MAN: Hey. *(Looking around)* Where're the kids?

WOMAN: Oh, you know, around. Cody Jr.'s at a play date. Baby's asleep.

MAN: Great. That's nice... *(Another hug)* Hi.

CODY: Shit. *(Beat)* Don't mind me...

(They laugh at this—not CODY, *of course, but the* MAN *and the* WOMAN. *They break their hug, and she goes back to setting up drink cups. The* MAN *tries to help out.)*

MAN: Sorry. It's just...

CODY: What?

MAN: I dunno. Great to see you guys...I mean, *both* of you.

CODY: Yeah? Well, then, you better get over here and gimme a big cuddle, too, while you're at it. I don't wanna be left outta the *lovefest.*

(The MAN *chuckles, then decides to call* CODY's *bluff. He moves toward the grill, but* CODY *holds up his chef tools in a makeshift cross.)*

MAN: ...I luv you, man.

CODY: Get the fuck outta here!

(CODY *and the* MAN *pretend to hug, then back away from each other. The* WOMAN *smiles at this as she starts on the plastic cutlery.)*

CODY: ...and you didn't bring your cards, I see.

MAN: Oh, damn! Sorry. You want me to run back over and...

CODY: Nah, we can do it later. What took you so long? *(Checks his watch)* It's already ten after...

MAN: Oh, yeah, sorry...I was finishing up this movie. On T V. Had to let it wrap up...that's the best part.

CODY: What, the end?

MAN: Uh-huh.

WOMAN: Why, to see what happens?

MAN: Well, sure, yeah...but to see who ends up with whom. How they all get paired off. The characters, I mean...

WOMAN: Oh. Right...

CODY: ...*okay*...

MAN: No, seriously...I love that. Trying to guess who'll end up together. Or if. *If* they will. As a writer, I find it really interesting...

CODY: Cool. *(Beat)* You want steak or some chicken? I got burgers, too.

MAN: Ummm...maybe a little of each. That all right?

CODY: Yep. Same thing I'm doing. High on the protein. No carbs...

MAN: Great.

(CODY *turns to a covered plate and begins taking off the foil to get at the meat. The* MAN *decides to return and help the* WOMAN. *He picks up a pitcher and starts pouring drinks.)*

WOMAN: ...so, what was on? The TV, I mean.

MAN: Oh, it was this Hitchcock thing…

WOMAN: Nice. Which one?

MAN: No, it was a, like, some tribute or something. On cable…

WOMAN: Oh.

MAN: All weekend. They're playing a *ton* of his films… one right after the other. It's pretty great.

WOMAN: I like Hitchcock…I think Cody does, too. Don't you, honey?

CODY: What's that?

WOMAN: Like Hitchcock movies…

CODY: Not much. They're all right. *The Birds* was good… *(Beat)* Anyways, I thought you were some *playwright*, so why the hell you spend all day in front of the movies?

WOMAN: …anyway… *(To the MAN)* Let's—

MAN: You liked *The Birds*, huh, Cody? That sounds suspiciously like you having *fun*…

CODY: Yeah, time 'a my life…

(CODY slaps some meat on the grill, seasons it, and puts down the lid. Opens the little steam valve.)

WOMAN: And what were you watching? I mean, before you came over…

MAN: Oh, right. Yeah, I was finishing up *Strangers on a Train*. Tonight is *Vertigo*, and this morning was that one with, ummm…*Shadow of a Doubt*. Plus, there's one of the lesser ones later, at midnight.

WOMAN: Really? Which one…I like him, maybe I'll watch it.

CODY: You already said that. Said you liked Hitchcock already…

WOMAN: I know, I was just—

CODY: ...just so you do. Know.

MAN: It's, umm, *Marnie.* I think.

WOMAN: Oh. Good.

CODY: The one about the liar... *(Beat)* I'm gonna go get the veggies.

WOMAN: ...check on the baby, would ya?

(CODY nods and heads off toward the kitchen—any of the exits will do. We just need to get him offstage. The MAN stops him.)

MAN: ...you mean "thief".

CODY: What?

MAN: She's a thief, in the film. *Marnie.* Or, Tippi Hedren is, the actress. She's a thief in that one...

CODY: Oh, I thought she was both. Anyway, same difference...*philosophically* speaking.

MAN: Really? How's that?

CODY: She steals shit, right?

MAN: Yeah...

CODY: Well, liars just steal the truth... 'S the same thing. It's all theft.

(And with that, CODY exits. The MAN and WOMAN are left looking at each other—that's okay, they don't mind. An easy smile between them)

MAN: ...man's got a point.

WOMAN: He always does—he is happy to tell you. *(Whispers)* And it usually has to do with his *mother*...

MAN: Ahhh, right. *(Beat)* Well, too bad they didn't offer a "philosophy" course at school...he might've aced it.

WOMAN: Probably. He does always get what he wants…

MAN: Yeah?

WOMAN: Oh, yeah. Always.

MAN: Even you? I mean…

(The WOMAN *looks hard at the* MAN, *unsure how to respond. She looks back at the house, then moves over toward him.)*

WOMAN: …no. He got me because I wanted him to. That's how.

MAN: Really?

WOMAN: Yes. From that first time I saw Cody…on the bus. The activity bus home one night. Right from then.

MAN: …wow.

WOMAN: Uh-huh.

MAN: That's so…great. Really.

WOMAN: Why? Why is that great?

MAN: Oh, you know, because…it's true love and all that. Right?

WOMAN: …you sure it's not just because I like a nice, thick black cock? Hmm? Maybe that's why…

(The WOMAN *tries to smile but has to look away, blushing. The* MAN *stops for a moment, as if stunned by this. He then moves down center. Toward us)*

MAN: …okay, obviously she didn't say it like that. I mean, it's obvious, right? She's not that way, would never say a thing like that…God, can you picture *her* saying that?! *Any*thing like that? *(Laughs)* No way, not at all. Or any girl, really. Not any that I know. Maybe, like, in a *movie* or something, but real people? Uh-uh. *But*, see…it is what *I'm* thinking right now. Or then. I mean, what I've had in my head since the first time

I heard about her and Cody. Or anytime you see a white girl and a…well, you know. And it is a cliché, I'm aware of that, but it's hard not to…I mean, most everybody knows those jokes, or stories, or whatever you wanna call 'em. And so I can't help it if that's what I'm imagining right now…I can't! And anyhow, a cliché is just a thing that's true, usually. Some true thing that gets said over and over… *(Beat)* But no, she never said that. Or will. Or will *ever*. Not her. Not Belinda Rivers. That was her maiden name…Rivers. I bet she's never said that before. "Cock." Not even lying in bed, with him, or…Jesus, he may be the only guy she's ever laid in bed with! I mean, it's possible. Shit, that's…whoah. Could you imagine? Damn. *(Beat)* Anyway, we need to be careful here, be as true to this as we can, so, no…she'd never say that. About Cody's, you know…*thing*. That was all me. Not that *I* was thinking about his—you know—just that…o-kay, let's drop it…

(The MAN *shrugs and returns to the picnic table, back there next to the* WOMAN, *who is turned and lost in thought. Just like we left her. Well, that's convenient.)*

MAN: That's so…great. Really.

WOMAN: Why? Why is that great?

MAN: Oh, you know, because…it's true love and all that. Right?

WOMAN: …people don't really use those words anymore, do they? I mean, not in a long time…

MAN: No. I s'pose not. But it's a nice thought all the same…

(The WOMAN *stands and goes to check the grill. She lifts the lid and turns the pieces of meat one by one. The* MAN *rises to stand near her.)*

WOMAN: …I wanted to be noticed. That's what it was.

MAN: Hmmm?

WOMAN: The reason I first…oh, nothing.

MAN: No, go ahead. Please.

WOMAN: When I said yes to Cody, the time he asked me out—bowling or to the skating rink, I don't remember now—I said okay because I thought it would make me stand out.

MAN: Really?

WOMAN: Sure. That's the problem with high school— one of the *many* problems, anyway. You're so desperate to fit in, and at the same time totally needing to stand out…

MAN: Exactly. Yeah, I mean…yes.

WOMAN: You know? And for me, well…I guess I never really stopped. Doing this, I mean, marrying Cody and staying here—if you could've seen my dad's face!— it's sad, really. Not sad, I suppose, but…pathetic, almost. That I need people to be aware of me that badly. Doesn't matter what you look like or how smart you are. No. It's really how you feel about yourself. Who you are. And I was raised with the total sense that I wasn't good enough…or that I wouldn't make the right choices. That's it. My parents were always nervous that I'd make some mistake along the way, even in preschool! And so, at some point…that is what I decided to do. Prove 'em right. I made a "mistake" they'd never forget. *(Beat)* But I was in love, too. I shouldn't sound— well, actually I *shouldn't* be saying any of this, but—I loved him. Cody. When we got married. I really think I did…but, then, it didn't hurt that he was rich and black and different. Especially the last one. Rich, I don't care so much about. I mean, it's okay…and black, well, that wasn't such a bad thing, either. But different? Now, that's a good one...I like *different*. Or at least thought I did...

(*The* WOMAN *looks at the* MAN, *to gauge his reaction. He nods and looks back toward the house. They both do—hey, they're not stupid.*)

MAN: ...oh.

WOMAN: Yeah. "Oh." As in, oh-oh...

MAN: That's funny. I mean, *interesting.*

WOMAN: Not really.

MAN: But it's...is that true?

WOMAN: Yes. Mostly. Because doing that, marrying him, it made me different, too. And I still get some kind of thrill from it...walking into an Arby's or through Wal-Mart with these two brown children in tow. My little *pickaninnies*—that's what my parents call them—with their light-colored eyes. I do. I mean, it might be old hat in a place like New York or wherever, but around here...it's still a pretty big deal. *(Beat)* These faces turning 'round to get a look at us, the whispering, and me with this fat checkbook and my head all held up. Defiant. I don't even know why I like it so much. I just do...

MAN: Wow.

WOMAN: Yeah. "Wow." Scary...

MAN: No, it's...why? Why "scary"?

WOMAN: ...scary that I'm that needy.

(*The* WOMAN *looks at the* MAN, *and he trails off. Tries to smile*)

MAN: No, not at all... *(Beat)* Listen, this is going to sound lame, so I'm preparing you now, but...see, I always thought you stood out. Completely. I mean, so much...

WOMAN: Huh. Well…

MAN: Wow, that was even worse than I thought! I mean, seriously sad. Forgive me.

WOMAN: No way. I'm keeping that…it's all mine.

MAN: What?

WOMAN: Just that, you know, little tidbit. You put it out there, so I get to have it…and thank you.

MAN: "Pleasure"—he says, glancing around to see if the husband is about to plunge a steak knife into his back…

(The MAN and the WOMAN both laugh at this—good, that's nice. Just like before.)

WOMAN: …I think you're in the clear. For a minute, anyway.

MAN: That's all I need. A minute. I'm much faster than I used to be…

WOMAN: Yeah, but he'll kill ya out in the open. It's in the flats, that's the problem…

MAN: Damn that Flyin' Cody Phipps!

(The MAN and the WOMAN laugh again—but they'd better be careful. CODY's coming. At the last moment, they both notice.)

WOMAN: Hey, sweetie!

MAN: Cody…you need any help?

CODY: Nah, I'm good… *(Beat)* Wouldn't wanna break up your *coffee klatch* there.

WOMAN: We were just…

MAN: …talking, you know…

CODY: Yeah, yeah, I know. I do know. Was watching you from the window there, in the kitchen, and…boy, you two are like a couple old nannies!

MAN: That's us!

WOMAN: I was checking the meat for you, and we just got to...

CODY: Funny, he never talks that much when I'm around. Does he?

MAN: *(Looking around)* Are you...I mean, do you mean *me*? 'Cause I'm standing right here.

CODY: I know *exactly* where you are. Believe me...

WOMAN: Honey, please don't...

CODY: Doesn't bother me. Not at all. You can knock yourselves out...I just noticed it. That's all.

(CODY takes a quick peek at the grill and then, satisfied, finds himself a nearby chair. He looks at the MAN and the WOMAN.)

CODY: ...carry on.

WOMAN: I think most of this is ready. Umm, maybe not the cutlets...

MAN: ...yeah, I think chicken's supposed to be—

CODY: Give it a minute. *(Beat)* So, what's up? What're you guys blabbing your heads off about? Hmm?

WOMAN: Oh, just, you know...

CODY: Nope. I don't. I do not.

MAN: Just, stuff, really. Life stuff...

CODY: What's that mean?

MAN: I dunno. We were *chatting*, that's all.

CODY: But not about you, I'll bet. *(Beat)* Am I right?

MAN: What's that mean?

WOMAN: Cody, honey, let's just...would you check these burgers, please?

CODY: I said leave it. Shit. They're fine. *(To the* MAN*)*
I'm saying I could see you both yakking on out here
about shit, but my guess is…you didn't say a damn
thing about yourself.

MAN: Why do you say that?

CODY: 'Cause I've noticed it. Times we've been
together…like pulling *molars* outta your skull to get
anything at all personal…

(The MAN *backs away a little—I never really noticed it, but
maybe* CODY's *right about him. The* MAN *sits at the table.)*

MAN: …that's true. I'm not the most open guy around.
Yeah.

CODY: Well, that's big of you…

MAN: Cody, look…

WOMAN: …sweetie…

CODY: No, seriously. I know ya know about us, ya
leave your damn *windows* open all day and night—
but I don't got hardly two bits of info on you. Was a
lawyer. Has a kid. That's it…

WOMAN: I'm turning the grill off…

(The WOMAN *does so. She starts moving the meat from the
metal rack inside the grill to a large serving plate. The* MAN
takes a drink, then smiles at CODY.*)*

MAN: …because those're the highlights. Honestly, not
much to tell.

CODY: Bullshit. Everybody's got a story. *Every*-body…

MAN: 'S that right? What's mine, then? I mean, if
you're so sure and all…

WOMAN: Guys, can we just…?

MAN: No, it's okay. It's fine. He's got something he
wants to say, so we should probably just hear it…

CODY: Yeah?

MAN: Go for it.

CODY: 'Kay… Well, let's see. You told us about your daughter. Not much, but some. *Enough.* Enough to know that's not the sore spot…

MAN: Did I forget to trim your hedges or something? I mean, Cody, what is up with this…?

CODY: Nothing. Just playing with you…

MAN: No, you're not. Uh-uh. You've got a thought, so let's hear it. *What?*

CODY: …all right. Fine. *(Beat)* Why're you really back here? And none of your smart-mouth answers…why did you stop being a lawyer? That's not something people really do. Give up a good job like that. Not usually.

(The MAN *looks long and hard at* CODY, *then over at the* WOMAN. *She's making herself a burger, but she's listening. No doubt about that)*

MAN: …I just did, that's all. Okay? Just up and quit one day, had my fill of it and walked out. Cleared out my things, and I was…done.

CODY: Huh…pretty generic. *(Beat)* Plus, a theater writer and living out *here*? I don't think so.

MAN: Writers can live anywhere, Cody. That's kind of the *point*…

(Both CODY *and the* WOMAN *watch the* MAN, *realizing that he doesn't wish to go any further. In a way, though, he needs to. This is the right moment.)*

WOMAN: …don't feel like you have to…

CODY: Don't do that. All right? Don't just always jump in to defend every damn person I have a conversation with. It is pretty fucking annoying... *(Beat)* The guy can just tell me to shut up, if he wants...

WOMAN: I know that. I *know.* I only wanted to make this nice, have some food out on the lawn. I'm sorry...

(CODY and the WOMAN stare each other down—to her credit, the WOMAN is holding her own.)

MAN: ...no, Cody's right. That's a total crock—company-line shit. I had to sign a statement, actually, that I would tell that story, or something like it, as what happened, so I got used to it, I guess. Yep. *(Beat)* But you guys, well...you're friends of mine, right? I can tell you the truth. Sure. *(To the WOMAN)* Do you mind if I have one of the burgers?

(The WOMAN nods, starts fixing him one. The MAN watches her as he talks; the WOMAN brings one each to the MAN and to CODY.)

MAN: ...I was let go. "Fired", I guess, is the term they used to use when our fathers were alive. Well, maybe not your father, Cody, because he was a self-made guy, but my old man was a mechanic, worked at that Union 76 over on McHenry all his life, and if he screwed up—like, totally ruined somebody's car or mouthed off to the owner—then he would get fired. He wasn't, no... but I was. Me. I was fired. For something I did.

WOMAN: ...I think I'm going to go inside.

MAN: No, please don't. Okay? I want you to hear this, Belinda. Need you to. Because I haven't really told anyone, so it feels good. Not *good*, but you know... freeing, somehow.

WOMAN: Are you sure you...?

CODY: Just let the man talk.

MAN: Thanks. Yeah. Well, does everybody have what they want, for lunch, I mean? Because after this, we

may not be…just checking. *(Beat)* I was a good lawyer,
fair, anyway. I was very fair with people, and decent.
And that's not an easy thing, in that job. Not at all, but
I was. Anyhow, I'm on a business trip one time, with
some of the people from my office, we were going to,
ummm, Pittsburgh or someplace, I don't remember,
but we're late for the plane—it was on United, I recall
that, it was with United. And I got there a little late,
maybe twenty minutes before the flight closed, but a
friend, this dude I knew from law school, is up there
getting his boarding pass, and he lets me slip in. Into
line. Ahead of a few other colleagues…and one of
them, this lady named Carol, an African-American
woman who worked with us, says something out loud.
Not a big deal, like, "Hey, no cuts", or something, but
you know, the kind of day it was, all rainy and a race
through the terminal, I just wasn't in the mood. Not at
all. Yet I let it go. I do. I get my thingie and even use
some miles to get' bumped up—the last guy to be able
to do it, they are totally sold out—and off we go, my
buddy and me, down toward security and to the gate.
I make eye contact with ol' Carol on the way, toss her
a smile, and we're off. Actually, we stop by Mickey D's
and grab a McRib each. Those're really good…

(The MAN *takes a breather;* CODY *and the* WOMAN *are
still there, hanging on his words.* CODY *heard the "African-
American" thing, and his antennae are up.)*

CODY: …where's this going?

WOMAN: Honey, he's trying to—

CODY: I'm just asking.

MAN: I'm sorry, I'm rambling. Lemme just get to the…
we get on the plane. So, we're sitting there in first,
having our pretakeoff ginger ale or whatever, and
people are filing past, bashing into me—I'm on the
aisle—with their two bags each, and we're talking

away, and bam!, I get tagged again by some computer
case. Right on the elbow. And it hurts, it really does,
so I'm about to say something...when I glance up, it's
Carol. Not even looking. Heading back into economy—
thanks to me, in all probability—and it just makes my
associate and me start laughing. I mean *howling*, really,
the two of us, there in the cabin.

At some point, I'm not sure when, a bit later—I
thought a *lot* later, but—I lean over to him, I lean in a
bit and say, really whispering, "Well, at least they still
sit in the back of the bus". Just for fun, right? It's this
little joke, we're on an Airbus, after all, and I swear to
God, the place goes silent. Like a church for a moment,
when the A/C is about to switch over or something...I
say this thing and a bunch of folks are suddenly
looking right down at me. Including *Carol*. See, some
old lady back there is messing around with her
suitcase, this old Samsonite, and the line hasn't moved.
Carol is, I mean, she is standing *right* there. Shit...I
start to sputter, try to stand up, my belt is hooked, and
it jerks me back into my seat, I spill the drink. A whole
parade. I do finally get to my feet and try to explain,
say, "What I meant to say was..." and she tears into
me, well, it was pretty unbelievable. 'S like *Angela
Davis* has suddenly appeared, and she's all waving
her hands and screaming at me—you know how black
women can get—with the "motherfuckin' " this and
that, like she'd never been to school a day in her life!
And I...I lost it. I admit it, I just totally lost it there for
a bit...and I grabbed her by both her shoulders, this
Carol woman, not hard or anything, but grabbed her
and shook her a second. I shook her and said, "Hey,
Carol, stop it! Stop acting like some *blue-gummed chimp*,
just fell outta the tree!" *(Beat)* So...just imagine what
the next five minutes were like, those last few moments
when I'm standing and collecting my stuff...it was just
so unreal. No, *sur*real. I will never forget that feeling...

And I didn't apologize, that's the thing. Which is
what really does me in, I guess. See, they wanted this
formal letter of…anyway, I just wouldn't do it. I wasn't
gonna back down. I was *defiant.* The firm "let me go"
about three days later. Well, I guess suspended first,
but then…yeah. My wife left a few weeks after that.
Not because it bothered her, I don't think, but because
it was the *right* thing to do. Or gave her an excuse,
anyway. This was almost a year ago. And *that* is who
you are renting your apartment to. *(Beat)* Anyway,
Cody, how's that burger?

(CODY *takes another bite before he says anything. Maybe
two)*

WOMAN: Maybe we should…I don't know. What
should we do now? Cody?

(CODY *wipes his mouth with one hand, then finds his
napkin. Uses it. Stands)*

CODY: Me? I'm gonna go check out the dish…maybe
that *Hitchcock* movie you're both so excited about.

MAN: You did ask…

CODY: Yeah, I know. Don't mean you always gotta tell
the truth.

WOMAN: Cody, we still have all this…

CODY: Then wrap it up. Save it for the kids, I don't give
a damn…

MAN: Maybe I'll head back over to—

CODY: No, you guys have a nice chat. Go on. Like
nothing happened. And it didn't, right? Nothing
happened. Other than we found out what a piece of
shit we got living here with us…

(The MAN *starts to say something, then stops. The* WOMAN
moves to CODY, *but he shakes her off. Holds up a finger)*

CODY: *(Toward the* MAN*)* ...you need to get gone. Outta this place. Right? End of the month.

*(*CODY *wanders off toward the house. Exits. The* MAN *and the* WOMAN *sit quietly for a moment. Maybe even longer— no hugs this time. Just silence. Then, out of nowhere, her hand touches the* MAN*'s hand. She holds it. Now, this is interesting.)*

WOMAN: ...well. I'm sure he's—I mean, he usually doesn't stay mad long...

MAN: Doesn't matter.

WOMAN: No?

MAN: Uh-uh. Glad I said it. Needed to.

WOMAN: Then good. People should do what they need to do. Mostly.

MAN: Yeah. *(Stands)* I'm gonna go back upstairs, is that okay?

WOMAN: Oh, please. Sure. Yes. I'll just...I'm gonna clean some of this up.

MAN: Do you want any...?

WOMAN: No, I'm fine. Absolutely.

MAN: 'Kay. Sorry.

WOMAN: No, don't be, it's...it was only *lunch*, right?

MAN: Right. I'll see you, then.

WOMAN: You, too.

MAN: Later.

(The MAN *moves off, down toward us. The* WOMAN *remains and clears the table.)*

MAN: ...so, that was different, huh? Very. Hey, maybe that'll make her like me more or something. She says she likes *different*. And I am that, if nothing else... *(Beat)* Speaking of Belinda, and I should've done this

earlier, but…hey. One thing you should know—or
should've known—about us. We did kiss once. Yes. I
don't mean in the past, not at the *drive- in* or anything,
but recently. Like, within the last few weeks. Not a big
deal, I mean, it was very nice, don't get me wrong…but
it was just this small little thing. It was. Or will be. Out
on the lawn here one time, when I'm cutting the side
yard. I was—or will be—ahh, mowing, like I said, or I
guess…maybe I was raking at that point. Yeah, raking,
and… *(Beat)* …we kiss. That's pretty much it. Just
this nice kiss that comes from her bringing me a glass
of tap water, something to cool me off. Didn't work!
Not after…not after doing that. With her. I wasn't or
will not be—I am not cool after that! And it's out of
nowhere, that's the thing that really knocks me out…
we just kiss. We kiss like there's a respirator between
us and our lips are the only thing keeping the other
person going. You know how that is, when you're with
someone and you get a bit close, sort of begin to cross
the *demilitarized zone* and there's no going back…that's
how it went. Amazing.

(The MAN *drifts for a moment, remembering it. Let's give
him some space—it sounds like it was kind of great. We
probably should've shown it before, but too late now. Or is
it?)*

MAN: But hey…if you guys wanna see, we can
probably show you. The kiss, at least. The thing itself.
It's a bit weird, to do it over again, I mean, you know,
after all the other stuff that you've…but we can pull it
off. No problem. Here.

(The MAN *takes off his shirt, pitches it out of the way. Finds
a weed- eater somewhere onstage—that's the designer's
problem. He starts working on the feeder [where the fishing
line comes out of the thing], and suddenly, the* WOMAN
appears. Glass of water in her hand. Ice cubes. He looks up.)

*(She smiles at him, holding up the drink. He takes the
tumbler and gulps down the cool liquid. She smiles and,
without thinking, reaches over and wipes his brow. He
smiles back. And then they're kissing—kind of surprising,
but believe me, it's happening. This goes on for a few
moments. When they stop, she leans over and steals a sip
from the glass. Moves off)*

(The MAN *watches her go. Wistful. Unsure. He shakes it
off and looks back at us. Starts changing his clothing—he's
going to need some jogging stuff. Sweats. Shoes. Nothing too
fancy)*

MAN: ...see, I told you—it was pretty nice. I don't
know if you could tell that from where you guys're
sitting, but...it was really so damn nice. *(Beat)* There's a
name for that area there, way up in the last rows...you
know what it is? It's slang, but it's funny as hell! Check
it out sometime, it's in that *Oxford* dictionary. I'll give
you a clue. It's under "N". *(He stretches now, shaking
out his limbs. Trying to loosen up a bit)* ...you know,
while we're gettin' so fancy—like, back in time and all
that—we should probably take a look at something
that happened a while ago. I mean, not as long ago as
the kiss, not that far back, but before now. Or before
now later, when this part happens. Right? Anyway, it's
worth checking out, 'cause it definitely puts a wrinkle
in things. Yeah, adds a little... Well, you'll see.

*(*CODY *enters, wearing running gear again and sweating
through it. Sits down and starts stretching out.)*

MAN: Cody and I met up once...over at this nature
preserve where they have these running trails. A mile
or so from here. A few weeks after the whole lawn-
party thing. We hooked up and went for a jog. This is
how it goes...

(The MAN *wanders over near* CODY *and drops down, starts his own form of stretching. Gradually,* CODY *glances at him.)*

MAN: ...hello. Hey.

CODY: What's up?

MAN: Not much.

CODY: All right. Here...

*(*CODY *stands up and unzips a large pocket on the front of his windbreaker. Pulls out a business envelope and hands it over to the* MAN. *The* MAN *opens it, counting out a stack of bills.)*

CODY: ...'s your deposit.

MAN: Uh-huh. *(Stops)* Kind of *niggardly*, isn't it?

CODY: Would you can it with that shit? It is not funny...

MAN: I'm joking! It's a *joke*... *(Beat)* You know what the word means, don't ya?

CODY: Yeah, I do. I understand, but that don't make it cool.

MAN: Okay, sorry, *(Taps his leg)* You're not gonna take anything out for my changing the *carpet*?

CODY: Ha-ha. Real cute...

MAN: Just asking.

*(*CODY *shakes his head; the* MAN *smiles and jams the thick wad of money into his warm-up pants. He reaches into another pocket and produces a single baseball card inside a thick plastic case. Hands it to* CODY, *who marvels at it and pops it into his front pocket. Zips it closed)*

CODY: Thanks... *(Beat)* I don't like this. I don't like meeting up out here...wanna be careful.

MAN: Fine. That's all right. I just needed some cash...

CODY: Whatever.

MAN: Had to rent a new place, buy a few *knickknacks*, that sort of thing...moving's not easy.

CODY: Good. Well, now you've got a little spending money.

MAN: Thank you. Thanks, Cody.

CODY: Yeah, yeah. Right.

MAN: That means a lot to me...

CODY: Just shut up, okay? Really...don't. *(Beat)* So, are we good?

MAN: Yep.

CODY: Fine. *(Beat)* ...How many times've you seen her now? I mean, since then. That day.

MAN: A few. Six, maybe...

CODY: Six? She's called you *six* times?

MAN: Something like that...and yes, I make sure she calls from the *house*. Leaving a paper trail...

CODY: Fine. Okay. And you've met...?

MAN: ...a couple.

CODY: I don't want to know any more than that.

MAN: Great.

(CODY shakes out his limbs, getting ready to run.)

CODY: ...but you guys aren't...I mean, you haven't, umm...right? Not yet.

MAN: That's really...not your business. Isn't that what we discussed? That was up to my discretion...

CODY: No, yeah, true, I was just...

MAN: ...believe me, it's better not to. *I'm* the one used to be the lawyer, remember?

CODY: 'Course I do. It's the only reason the two of us are even standing here. *(Beat)* How much longer, you figure?

MAN: What, until you can say something? Or catch us? Hell, I dunno…give it a month or so. Don't ya think?

CODY: Yeah. That's…I s'pose.

MAN: You seem anxious…

CODY: Of course I am. Come on!

MAN: Of course you are… *(Beat)* Who is she, by the way?

CODY: What?

MAN: The girl I saw you with…out by the reservoir. Last week. She's cute, but really young.

CODY: No, that's the…I'm training her. She's on the track team at—

MAN: *Right.* Look, I know you've told the wife that you're in love with your work, I know that—she told me as much—but please, Cody, do me the favor. I'm a *guy.* I can smell *chick* on you a mile away…

CODY: No, seriously, I'm not…no.

MAN: Hey, whatever it takes to sleep at night. Knock yourself out.

CODY: I don't know what you're saying…

MAN: I'm saying, pretty outright, that a person does not do this, this *Mayor of Casterbridge* thing you've got going here, without some reason. A reason like the one I saw you out running with.

CODY: No, shit, that is…it's not anything. I just wanted to get this Jackie Robinson card back, so I…

MAN: Cody, please. Be honest here. You did not ask me to go in with you on this racket, our little shell game we're running, just so you could put some piece 'a *cardboard* back into your collection... *(Beat)* You asked me to take your wife—have her in *trade*—if I'd help you pull it off. For shit like that, I mean, *that* elaborate...there is always a reason.

CODY: No, we just got to talking...I mean, at the airport...we got to talking about that card and then, I dunno, we...

MAN: Cody, I was *there*, remember? Right there next to you. You asked me this flat out. Told me your story. The "disgruntled hubby, the trophy wife", the whole damn business.

CODY: Yeah, but I knew you liked her...back in school, I'm saying. I came to you because I was...because...

MAN: No, I *came* up to you...saw you and made the connection, came over and, like, *three* beers later...you dish up this proposition. A *whopper* of a proposition...

CODY: I'd just been thinking, that's all! Thinkin' about it. *(Beat)* You did always like her. I know that...

MAN: So, you were just being nice, then? Gonna let me have her as a *gift*?

CODY: No, I...

MAN: You gave me your wife. *Asked* me to take her. Now, you're either *Henny Youngman*, or there's something fishy going on! *(Beat)* I'm only saying this to help remind you—do not forget the truth here. The truth is always of some importance.

(CODY stares at the MAN, not sure how he knows all this. Suddenly, the MAN seems a lot sharper than he's come off during the rest of the proceedings.)

CODY: ...you must've been a damn smart lawyer.

MAN: I was okay. Just all right. I didn't have the stomach for it. So?

CODY: So, yeah…yes. Her. She's…I do not need people knowing about that. She's in school, and I don't—

MAN: Good. I just want to know the how and why of it. Nothing more.

CODY: Fine. That's fine. That is a long-term project. My *own* business.

MAN: Yes, it is. Keep it that way, okay? You've hidden it this long, do not screw it up now… *(Looking around)* I don't like standing here, just yakking away like this. Maybe we should jog…

CODY: What…you and me?

MAN: Yeah. Makes it look all natural. Just like two "buddies" out for a run. Keepin' in shape.

CODY: I'd kill you in a race…

MAN: I didn't say "race". I said "jog". You've got *race* on the brain, my man…

CODY: You just don't stop, do ya?

MAN: Hey…by any means necessary. Isn't that what you people always say?

CODY: Stop! Come on, dude, knock it off.

MAN: Okay…

(CODY *and the* MAN *begin to "jog" —basically running in place, but we'll work that out as we go. They move in silence for a bit, then start to talk again.)*

CODY: By the way…that shit about the woman on the plane was not funny. At all.

MAN: Hah! Sorry 'bout that…spur-of-the-moment thing.

CODY: Yeah, well…

MAN: It worked, didn't it?

CODY: Yes, it worked. Worked at pissing me off, that's what it did…

MAN: Listen, we could've gone on like that, me living upstairs and typing away, sneaking glances at the Mrs for the next *eight* months. I made a move, did a little jump-start, that was all…

CODY: You didn't have to go there…say bullshit like that.

MAN: Cody, it was a perfect step, okay? Per-fect. While you were in getting the kabobs, Belinda told me a story out there, something about her that made me feel that I should make a play like that…and it worked.

CODY: I hate that kinda thing, just so you know. Any kind of racist shit. Just so you're aware…

MAN: I know. Of course I know. That's *why* I did it…

CODY: I need her out of my home, but I don't wanna go through all this crap to do it. Otherwise, fuck, I might as well just get a *divorce*…

MAN: Hey, you *are* going to get divorced! You'll have to…you're just going to get everything that you want *in* the divorce. That's why I'm here.

CODY: …right…

MAN: Isn't that what we agreed to?

CODY: Yeah. It is.

MAN: All right, then. So don't let a tiny bit of prejudice get in the way of what we're doing… *(Beat)* That thing on the plane happened. I just never lost my job over it. I said it, had a good laugh with my co-worker, and enjoyed a first-class dinner all the way to Pittsburgh. I'm not a lawyer anymore because I decided to get back into writing, that's all. I am not married now because it didn't work out—I was a liar and a mediocre husband—but I'm gonna try harder next time. *And* I don't see my kid that often because she's a girl and, frankly, I'm just not that into it. *(Beat)* That's all there really is to my story...

CODY: Oh.

MAN: Yep. "Oh." As in oh-oh...

CODY: What?

MAN: Nothing. Just something I heard...

(CODY and the MAN stop running for a moment. Make that, the MAN stops [holding his side], and CODY holds up for him.)

CODY: Tired?

MAN: Yeah, hold on a sec, lemme catch my breath.

CODY: You gotta push through the pain...

MAN: ...you gotta back off for a minute, let me worry about my own self.

CODY: Once a fatty, always a fatty. Ya probably got a weak heart. Kidneys.

(The MAN takes in a few deep breaths, trying to fight off a cramp. Flips CODY the finger. CODY wanders about, keeping warm and stretching.)

MAN: ...hey, we can't all be Olympians. Or *almost* Olympians.

CODY: Whatever.

MAN: I mean, you did nearly make it, right? That's what I heard.

CODY: Something like that...

MAN: Not that I used to search all over the Internet for news of the past or whatnot, but...you know.

CODY: Yeah.

MAN: Word gets around.

CODY: Great.

MAN: So what happened? You were good.

CODY: Uh-huh. Well, "good" don't mean shit. Not out there. Not in sports.

MAN: True.

CODY: Plus, I never even really...come on, you probably heard the whole damn story.

MAN: No, seriously, what? I mean, I knew you went off to school on some big scholarship, but that's all I—

CODY: Right. *(Beat)* Well, I...I hit a bad patch at college. Yeah. 'S what my ol' man called it. "A rough spot."

(The MAN doesn't seem in any hurry to get back to it, so CODY paces around. Thinking)

CODY: ...I threw a race once, qualifying for nationals. This one race. Well, not *threw*, exactly, no, I guess I didn't "throw" it, 'cause to do that you'd have to lose, and I didn't. Nope. See, I won...won it, but I wasn't supposed to.

MAN: Really. That's... So what was the, you know...? I don't follow.

CODY: ...it was this... *(Considers it)* ...nothing. Forget it.

MAN: No, what? Come on...

(CODY squats down near the MAN now, remembering.)

MAN: ...they wanted me to be a rabbit for 'em, my freshman year. And not even my event! I was done for the day with two firsts, but they asked me to take off quick in the five thousand and tire the other teams out, help our guys out— something to do with building my character and shit like that, *unity*—but I was like, "Fuck this", and took off running. Never looked back. I beat all 'a those motherfuckers. *(Smiles)* Guess I'm not cut out for "team" sports…which I never knew track was till I got to college.

(CODY *stops a second, recalling the moment. The* MAN *watches.)*

CODY: Anyways, I lost all my scholarships 'cause I would not apologize or back down. "Accept responsibility", I think they called it…and, you know, that's what folks wanna talk about in the end. To *dwell* on. Me being defiant. But my winning, they forgot all about that fact. Just like usual. People forget…

MAN: Huh. Wow…

CODY: Yeah, "wow"…and so that's what happened to the Olympics. That's as close as I ever got to any gold medal.

(*A long silence develops between* CODY *and the* MAN— *begrudging and respectful. These two may just be more alike than we first suspected.)*

(*After a moment,* CODY *moves to the* MAN *and presses a finger into his chest.)*

CODY: …so, what's the next step?

MAN: Whatever you want. Walk in on us at dinner or someplace…you decide.

CODY: No, I thought you said that—

MAN: Can we just play it by ear? I think it's gonna be better that way. More real…

CODY: Yeah, fine. *(Beat)* Just back off on the bigotry shit. Don't use that no more…

MAN: I'm not a *racist*, would you stop! I did it for the effect…you're the one keeps bringing it up.

CODY: I just don't want my kids hearing any of that.

MAN: …Ralph is *two*…

CODY: Cody Junior, then. I won't allow it.

MAN: What the hell do you think I'd say? Huh?! I
hardly saw 'em when I lived on your property, so...
relax.

CODY: It's hard enough out there, for a child like that.

MAN: Like what?

CODY: You know...he's...

MAN: See? You're the one doing all the segregating...
he's a little boy. He'll be fine! Parents break up all the
time, and the children bounce back. That's-their-job. To
bounce.

CODY: Okay...

MAN: ...it is interesting, though, about the kids. Kids
like yours. People always see you as these minorities,
right, but then you look at their skin and all that—the
children, I mean—and you guys're really the dominant
ones. It's true. All the nappy hair and the big lips and
shit...it always comes out on top, when your type gets
together with some white girl. You ever notice that? I
mean, not that anybody would *want* it, but it still does,
all the same. Sure, they've got Belinda's eyes, but all
the rest of it...'s straight from the *Congo*.

(CODY *is suddenly next to the* MAN, *right in his face. The*
MAN *doesn't back off, and* CODY *lets him have it—pushes
him hard on the chest, knocking him down. The* MAN *smiles,
starts to get up, then dives at* CODY's *legs. He brings* CODY
*down, and the two wrestle like a pair of Greco-Romans. It
gets kind of nasty. [Actors are free to add their own assorted
groans and fighting sounds here.] They finally release and
move away. Exhausted)*

(*The* MAN *stands up, wiping blood from his mouth with
a tissue and moving down toward us. He glances back at*
CODY.)

MAN: All right, I admit it, that part was just a
shameless attempt at a bit of action...little treat for

the "gun and knife" crowd. But hey, you need to have something for everybody, right? I mean, take a look at the Elizabethans, you don't believe me. You give 'em the ol' soliloquy here, you have 'em grab their crotch over there... 'S all about *balance*. It is. In reality, he pushes me, I push back...you know, it's one of those *guy* fights. Lotta noise, not so much happens. *(Beat)* Okay. So long as you know...

(The MAN *tucks his bloody tissue away and heads back to where* CODY *is sitting. Original tableaux—fancy name for same thing we just saw. After a long moment,* CODY *starts laughing. The* MAN *joins in.)*

CODY: ...you are a goofy fucker! Seriously. Just like back in school...

MAN: We aim to please...

CODY: Damn! I mean, shit, you're...crazy.

MAN: Depends on the day, Mister Phipps. On the day in question...

CODY: Yeah. But honestly, I don't want my kids hearing that...stuff.

MAN: I *understand* about the kids. And you want joint custody, right?

CODY: 'Course.

MAN: Not total, because she'll never go for that. But we can try to...

CODY: Whatever we gotta do. Just do it.

MAN: "Just do it." Nobody knows better than ol' Nike. She was a goddess, wasn't she? In the ancient days, I mean. *Nike.* I think that's where they got the, you know...logo...

CODY: Hell if I know. *(Studying him)* You really are one odd motherfucker...

MAN: Thank you. Compliment accepted…

CODY: Uh-huh. I need to go. Get myself off to work.

MAN: Cool. I'm meeting Belinda later.

CODY: Okay. *(He stops for a moment, then shakes his head. Laughs)* …man, that is just too strange. Being in on a thing like that…*happy* she's cheating on me.

MAN: We can stop. We can all go have us another *barbecue* if you'd like.

CODY: Funny. Real damn funny. Just do what you need to…

MAN: I will.

(CODY nods and starts off, heading back toward town. The MAN stops him with a last question.)

MAN: …what is it about her, though, Cody? That you hate so much?

CODY: What?

MAN: Just curious.

CODY: I don't… *(Beat)* No, I guess I do, actually. Hate 'er. Never thought of it that way, but yeah. I do.

MAN: So…?

CODY: I dunno. After a while, it's a bit of everything, I s'pose. Her face, the way she flosses her teeth, all that stuff. Browsing my mail and shit. Yeah. I mean, it's great at first. She always looked real nice against my skin, walking around town hanging off my arm. I used to love it, I mean, it was *cool*…going over and waiting in her living room, to go out. With her parents standing there! *(Beat)* And, yes, she is the mother of my kids and all, too, but after a while, you know…I guess the *novelty* of it just wore off.

MAN: …that's nicely put. Succinct.

CODY: Just trying to be honest.

MAN: So, why didn't you, then? Why not just leave, or...?

CODY: 'Cause I got a place here in this community to think about. A legacy and the boys and all kinds 'a crap. She divorces me, and everybody says, "See, I told ya so. Told you it wouldn't work out", and they leave it at that. But if I go, if *I'm* the one to take off, well, then, I'm just some uppity black boy, got no business being here. My stores'll close, lose the house. Everything. *(Beat)* The same reason my ol' man stayed...that guy hung in there, built his wife an empire. A goddamn *empire!* Dude weathered fuckin' El Nino and you know what? The people *respected* him. They did. They all understood he married a *cunt* and let it go at that...

MAN: ...but she's not at all like *your* mom, is she? Belinda, I mean. No matter what kind of crap you've thrown at her, she doesn't take off like your mother used to. Right? Hard as you try...

CODY: Don't. Do *not*...

MAN: ...which means she can never come crawling back, so you can forgive her. Like your father used to.

CODY: Dude...you just found yourself yet another topic to keep your fucking *paws* off of. I mean it.

MAN: It was just a guess...

CODY: Yeah, well, suck my dick...piece 'a shit like you talking about my *dad*.

MAN: No, thanks. I only eat white meat.

CODY: I can't wait till this thing is over.

MAN: Me, too.

CODY: Good.

MAN: ...'s a match made in heaven. She's making a point by staying, and so are you! Wow. You two are—

CODY: ...I'm outta here...fuck you.

MAN: You just keep your end of things up...I'll do the rest. Have a nice day...

(CODY *gives him the finger and walks off. Angry. The* MAN *turns away and moves back down toward us. Sheepish grin*)

MAN: ...hey, sorry for thatl Got a touch outta hand, so forgive me. I should explain. You really need to take a good look at the last few moments, decide for yourselves what happened there. I mean, how much is real... *(Beat)* It *happened,* that much I can tell you. We did meet, talked for a bit, he gave me an envelope. We even ran. And I told you what went on—or will— when we get into our little shoving match. But the rest? Well, hey, that stuff's for you to decipher. I can't help you out with everything, wouldn't be any fun! But you guys had to be expecting at least one exchange like what you just saw, right? I mean, at *least* one... some swearing, the digs at women. A crazy plot twist. You had to know that something like that was gonna transpire! Without it, this would all be just so damn, what? I dunno. *Ordinary,* I guess. People in and out of love. Trouble breaks out. Happens all the time— movies, on the T V, your neighbors next door. And I'll tell you, it's not so outlandish, either, what just went on. Not with all that junk you see on the news. People, they tire of each other, give up on what they've got instead of fixing it, or trying to. It's easier to just... start over, go online, bury themselves at the office. *Any*thing rather than get to the bottom of their own shit. We're weak, that's really what it is. We are lazy and pushy and we want it all today. Or sooner, even. Now. And as long as we get it, our fair share— or even a pinch more—well, then, who really gives a fuck what happens to anybody else? Right? *(He pulls that thick wad of cash out of his pocket, turns it over in his hands.)* ...this could be my deposit, what I gave them when I

moved in. Maybe. Or it's a payoff for me to take the
little missus off of Cody's hands. *Or* for that baseball
card, even! Hell…this *might* just all be going through
my head when I'm standing there at Sears, staring at
Belinda again for the first time. I mean, don't look at
me…I dunno where this damn thing is going, either! I
really don't. All I do know is, whether any of that stuff
you saw is real, the end result is this: I've started work
on a play—it's *this* story, *technically*, but I've changed
some of the situations around so that it's not…well, I
don't think anybody's gonna notice. And especially
not if it sells! *(Beat)* Belinda is with me now, out of their
house and living at my place. She's with the children
most days, at least for the moment, just until they settle
things, and Cody, well, he got what he wanted, too.
He did. He finally got—after all those hurtful years of
watching his dad take his mother back, time and time
again—Cody got a white woman to walk out on him
and stay gone. You should see him strutting around
town now, telling anybody who'll listen about what
Belinda did, and how hurtful it'll be on the kids and
having the time of his life. How she never would've
done this, something so humiliating to him, if he
wasn't *black*. Seriously, people have told me he's said
that very thing. "If I wasn't black." Yep, he's gone
and pulled the ol' Ace 'a Spades out, one last time…
wouldn't ya know it? *(Beat)* Also, I think maybe I came
off a little too, I dunno, *something*, in that last bit. Not
like myself. "I can smell chick on you a mile away." I
mean, come on! *(Laughs)* But then, people are so many
things, faces, in a given day, maybe that's just some
side of me, this other part, that doesn't get out that
often but is there. I dunno. But this time—'cause we're
about to finish this off right now—this time out I'll be
a bunch more like I was in the beginning. This is really
about them now, anyhow, settling up and the like…I'm

just there to be a support to her. To Belinda. Yep. I'm...
anyway...

*(Things should probably change here to something more
formal—what the hell does that mean? I don't know. But
we could use a desk, maybe, and a few chairs.* CODY *and the*
WOMAN *should already be seated, waiting. The* MAN *can
wander over in his own time. Soon, but you know what I
mean.)*

MAN: ...hello. Sorry that I'm...

WOMAN: It's okay, *(checks* CODY*)* I mean, *fine.*

MAN: Right, right..."fine but not okay". I remember.

WOMAN: Yes. That's...right.

(They sit in silence for a moment—make it a long one. CODY
glances around. Checks his watch)

CODY: Where *is* this guy? *(To the* MAN*)* You see
anybody out in the hall?

MAN: Ahh, no, I didn't. I was just...no.

CODY: Fine.

MAN: I'm sure he's coming...

CODY: Yeah? How do you know that?

MAN: Just hopeful. That's all...

WOMAN: Guys, let's not do this. Not right now...okay?

*(*CODY *grunts and goes back to staring at the wall; the* MAN
reaches over and squeezes the WOMAN's *hand. She smiles.)*

CODY: You two look over everything? The papers I had
sent over, and the...?

WOMAN: Yes. *(Looks directly at* CODY*)* You don't have to
involve him, this is really between us.

CODY: Hey, he's the one you're screwing now, so he
can—

WOMAN: I'm really not gonna sit here for that! I won't, Cody, I mean it.

CODY: Fine. I'll shut up…

MAN: …I doubt that…

CODY: Fuck off.

MAN: No, Cody, I don't want to. So I won't.

(CODY *and the* MAN *have one of those adolescent male stare-downs;* CODY *blinks first. Looks away. Checks his watch again*)

CODY: Two hundred bucks an hour, ya think he could be on time…

MAN: Right.

WOMAN: Yes. That'd be nice…

CODY: Man… *(Beat)* You did look at the stuff, though, right? I mean, all the changes from that last draft and the—

WOMAN: Yes, Cody, we read it over. *Both* of us.

CODY: Good. All right. And you're sure you want the single payment instead of the…?

WOMAN: Yes.

MAN: We do. Yeah. Better to just finish this off, clean, and we can all…you agree to the custody schedule, and we're fine with the settlement, *(Takes the* WOMAN's *hand)* We don't want your precious house or your stores, any of that crap. We'll manage…

CODY: From what, your *book deals*…?

WOMAN: Cody…

CODY: Just asking.

MAN: I *don't* write books. I'm writing a…look, don't worry about us, okay?

CODY: Whatever.

MAN: Seriously…

WOMAN: We're going to be happy. That's what's important. Something *we* never figured out, you and me…

CODY: That's bullshit, but think what you want.

WOMAN: I will. I'm gonna think and feel and do whatever I want from now on. And you can't do anything about it. You can't yell at me, or make faces behind my back, or turn Cody Junior against me anymore…

CODY: Oh, *please*…

WOMAN: You can't! You cannot do one damn thing to me…none of your silences or hitting or putting one of those dark fingers of yours anywhere near me. Not ever again. No, you are not *allowed*…

CODY: …you better watch it…

MAN: No, Cody, she doesn't have to…

CODY: I said to watch your mouths, man!! BOTH OF YOU!! Just watch that kind of fucking shit around me…

(CODY *stands up and slams his chair against the table, taking a step toward the* MAN. *The* MAN *remains seated, not engaging. That's probably best. The moment deflates, and* CODY *tries to save face—he heads for the door.*)

CODY: …I'm gonna go look in the hall, check on this motherfucker.

WOMAN: You do that.

CODY: I will.

MAN: So, go then. Do it.

(CODY *starts off, then looks back at the* MAN. *The* WOMAN, *too. A gleam in his eyes*)

CODY: ...but if I ever wanna trade back, you'll let me, right? Hmm?

(The MAN *stares at him for a moment, then slowly nods;* CODY *smiles and exits. The* WOMAN *watches him go, looking at the door. The* MAN *watches, too, until the* WOMAN *turns to him.)*

WOMAN: ...what's he mean by that?

MAN: Oh, ya know.

WOMAN: No, I don't. No. What?

MAN: He's, ummm, he's just...Cody's just trying to...

(The MAN *and the* WOMAN *look at each other, then the* WOMAN *glances at the door again. After a moment, the* MAN *rises and crosses to us.)*

MAN: Okay, sort of a dilemma here, right? Bit of a pickle...do I tell Belinda everything or make a run for it?

(The MAN *glances back at the* WOMAN, *then turns pleadingly to us for advice.)*

MAN: I'm serious, gimme some help here. I always imagined a day like this, one where she stumbles on to a cell-phone record or a scribbled note on a napkin and asks me about it...and I believe that I'd do the righteous thing. Tell her the truth. But the thing of it is, the truth is just so damn...elusive, isn't it? Like, I mean, *unknowable.* In the end. The second you start telling somebody what the truth is—how it goes—it all starts to slip away. Not, like, some lie, exactly, but close. This half-remembered version of one side 'a things. And what would the point be? I'll tell you this much—we end up pretty happy. Or will, however this time issue works itself out. We go and get married not too much later, even have ourselves a couple kids. Both boys, pleased to report. And we live happily ever after... or the equivalent of that, whatever that means today.

Yes, we disagree on occasion, I sleep in the guest room every now and then, one of the kids breaks an eardrum when he's swimming, but all in all, we survive. We make it as a couple, and that, my friends, is not easy. It is work. But I love it, I do, I love her…always have. And I can see it on her face, at night or when we're on the back patio, at that blue hour when the sun's just dropped down…she is finally at peace. So what the hell am I gonna tell her right now to ruin it all? Huh? Nothing, that's what…I'm gonna make up some tale about a baseball card I've promised him from my collection and go with that. Stick with it to my dying breath… *(Beat)* Quick story. The "Jackie Robinson" story. Cody gave me that card—it really is a nice one— if I'd go out with Belinda to the movies that one time. Time I mentioned way earlier. Remember? See, he was cheating on her, even way back then. He'd met this other girl, another cheerleader from over at Central, and he wanted to go out with her. That same night. So, he calls me, comes over, and tells me this whole tale about Belinda and how they're dating other people and shit and would I mind helping out? Cody tells me to go and pick her up at her house, six-thirty, and head over to the drive-in, this Showboat spot. He tells her the same thing— well, that I'm gonna pick her up, but—he'll meet us there, friends are joining us, I mean, the *usual* line of Cody Phipps bullshit. And that's how I end up seeing a movie with Belinda. One that she doesn't even remember going to. But I did get that card outta the deal. He was in a pinch, Cody was, and he agreed to it…screamed his head off, but yeah, he gave it to me. And this was the '52 Topps card with the red overlay. That thick smear of crimson on the backside— like a baboon's ass. Very scarce. But see, Cody was always so desperate to get into some white girl's pants that he'd part with something he really cared about. And that always made me hate him a bit—a little bit.

Because he picked on me…picked me to help him,
since I was no threat. Friendly and fat and always up
for whatever. A perpetual Bachelor Number Two.
I knew what he was doing, totally got it, but I liked
her so much, Belinda, that I was willing to…anyway,
that's the kind of guy Cody was. *(Beat)* See, Cody
Phipps was born a nigger. He still is, to this day. And
I do know the difference, believe me, between regular
black people and what Cody is. Oh yeah, absolutely.
I never really liked the guy—yes, back in school, I'd
hang with him, do some stuff, but basically just so
he wouldn't make fun of me or knock me around.
But Cody was always a nigger, even back then. This
lazy, mean-spirited coon who acted like everybody
owed him something. All that sort of post—Civil War,
Malcolm X, heavy-lidded bullshit that guys like him've
been trading on for years. Forty acres and a mule and
always ready to lay down the ol' Ace 'a Spades. Well,
hey, *man*, forgive us for dragging your sorry asses over
here, 'cause-it-wasn't-fuckin'-worth-it! *(Beat)* Now,
look…I don't really think in that way, use those terms
very often, because the good side of me, the *educated*
portion, says, "Hey, no, don't you do that, we're all
God's chillun", and so on. But see, raised like I was,
where I was—by *whom* I was— and that crap is always
right up there, near the surface, waiting to bubble over.
Cut me off in traffic sometime, you'll see what I mean!
(Beat.) And anyhow…it's just a word, right? "Nigger."
A word like any other. Only has power if you let it…

(The MAN *looks back at the* WOMAN—*she's still staring off.
Waiting for her cue. He looks back at us one more time.)*

MAN: But I'm not gonna screw this up…forget it. I'll
make up a lie—I'm a lawyer, don't forget, *ex*, so it
comes easy to me. Something. I'm not saying the other
stuff was at all true, that crazy shit about us trading or
whatever, but…we did see each other, Cody and I, at

the airport that one time. And if she knows that, finds that out, then it's only another step to realize that Cody might've mentioned the garage apartment and some of their problems and all the rest. Maybe. And I'm not gonna take that chance, because from there it's only a hop-skip to understanding that, yes, I may have used this, used *them* in some way…to get what I wanted. What I've probably always wanted. Belinda. I'll tell ya one thing, though—whether he was in on it or not— Cody was no idiot. Not ever. He could see what I was up to— slowly trying to take her away, away from him—and he did nothing to stop me. *Encouraged* it, even. So, that says something…it does. I still see him, Cody, some days around town. Running. Over past the golf course and down there. I don't think there's so many hard feelings anymore. Least I hope not… *(He looks over at the* WOMAN.*)* But I'll smooth this over, and we can get on to all that stuff I just told you about. That good stuff. I can't wait…to be with her. Finally. After all this time. It's taken a lot to get here, to this place, but it's all for the best, isn't it? Years of hatred and lies and betrayal that it took for Belinda and me to be together. For her to be happy. 'S worth it, though, right? Sure. I mean, *anything's* worth it, as long as you mean well…

(The MAN *smiles at us, then returns to his seat next to the* WOMAN. *He takes her hand, and she turns back to him.)*

WOMAN: …what did he mean, sweetie?

MAN: Nothing. It's a card, that's all. That stupid Jackie Robinson card he's been talking about…

WOMAN: The rare one?

MAN: Uh-huh.

(A quiet falls over them as the WOMAN *studies the* MAN. *She reaches out and touches his face. Softly)*

WOMAN: ...I know what you've done.

MAN: What? I mean—

WOMAN: I do. I'm not stupid, so I know...

MAN: I never said you were. *(Beat)* Okay, honey, what? Come on, *what?*

WOMAN: You gave it to him. Didn't you? That card.

MAN: Ummm, well...yeah. Yes, I did.

WOMAN: You felt bad, and you *gave* it to him...

MAN: I... Look, I did it for you. For *us.* I thought it might, you know. Help. To smooth things over...

WOMAN: Oh. *(Beat)* So, what's he wanna give you for it? I thought you were...

MAN: Just one of his players. His...

WOMAN: Yeah?

MAN: ...yes. One of his good ones.

WOMAN: Huh. You sure you want to? I mean, you love that thing...just don't let him *bully* you. Okay?

MAN: I know. I won't.

WOMAN: Because he can do that. Be a bully. And you've got a good heart, so...

MAN: It's fine. *(Smiles)* Promise.

WOMAN: All right, then. *(Beat)* You sure?

MAN: No, yeah. I'm sure. Very sure. Yep. Very...

WOMAN: ...okay.

(The WOMAN *smiles at the* MAN, *then looks straight out at us. He reaches over and kisses her on the cheek. Slowly turns out to the audience. They are together now, but lost in their own thoughts. Alone)*

(Silence. Darkness)

END OF PLAY

CPSIA information can be obtained
at www.ICGtesting.com
Printed in the USA
LVHW011517300721
694152LV00020B/542